This Journal Belongs To:

Name

Phone

Email

IF YOU FIND THIS JOURNAL
PLEASE CONTACT ME

The lives of people around the globe have been radically changed from using this guide and reading the Bible cover to cover!

"I have been a Christian my whole life, but I had never read the Bible cover to cover. Reading it starting from the beginning has given me a broader perspective of God's full picture and that He had a plan from the beginning to the end of time. He has always been faithful. Knowing that He has a plan has given me the freedom to step into the unique purpose He has for me in life. Get busy, get moving, and get in the Word and see what God has for you!" ~*Christina Stempke, CA*

"I have been reading the Bible for 58 years. I have started to read the Bible cover to cover so many times and never successfully finished it. Doing it in a group and having journal questions has allowed me the chance to finally get through all of the Bible. It helped me to dive deep. I never realized how much the Bible, old and new, go together. It has built my faith so strong through this whole process. I plan on doing it every year!" ~*Karen Sanchez Wright, CA*

"I love the Word just soaking through me. I listen to it mainly as I commute to and from my son's house to watch my grandchildren. I just let the Holy Spirit feed me. ~*Julie Bowen Stern, FL*

"Spending time with Him in His word has made me hungry for more and has grounded me. Plus, it has given me new understanding because He gives us the sight to "see" what He desires to reveal. Every season is different and it's beautiful how fresh the Word is every day. I had no idea how much I loved the Old Testament. Reading it today feels so relevant, and the joy of integration for meaning today created such light. His timing is perfect. I've found myself less self-reliant, and trusting God in faith this year reading the Bible consistently. My relationship with him is so much deeper, which pours out into my other relationships." ~*Janet Johnson, SC*

"My understanding of scripture has deepened. My relationship with God grows every day. I am more aware to offer mercy and grace to others. I am so thankful for this Bible study and the group I have been able to read the Bible with. I am sad to think about when it's over." ~*María López, PA*

"I have always wanted to read the Bible from beginning to end. The more I seek his Word the more I want to know and understand. I will be starting over again to see what I get out of it the second time around. Surprisingly, my husband wants to listen to it the next round. I think he sees how much I have grown in my search for God's word that he is feeling left out!" ~*Deb Gerken Thompson, ND*

"I have loved reading the scriptures! Love the restoration of the name in the Word and learning some Hebrew as well! His faithfulness has been amazing. Family relationships have been restored and so much more!" ~*Sonja Lee, WI*

"I have found so much goodness reading the Bible cover to cover. I love the Gospels! I have loved creating a habit of reading the Word and greater intimacy with the Father." ~*Savannah Dyer, CA*

"This Bible challenge has been amazing because the Bible has come alive in a whole new way for me! Even when I have gotten behind on my weekly reading, God has spoken to me so powerfully. Even in scriptures I previously thought were dull and boring, God spoke to me exactly what I needed to hear in that moment of my life. You are never really behind; God's timing is perfect. Just keep pressing forward." ~Jeanmarie Kaehler, WA

"My Bishop's wife first told me to start reading with the book of Psalms and later gave me other books to read, but never in order. This is the first time I have gone through the Bible like this. This study has revealed the Bible to me in a new and deeper way. I can see how everything is repeated at least once, and how the Old Testament and New Testament back each other up. And I am now seeing God's love throughout the Bible more than I ever have before." ~Sharilyn Garrett, MI

"This is my first time reading through the entire Bible. I have been blown away by so much! There is no new evil under the sun. God's mercy is great for His people. I have gained a new awe at what Jesus did for us in light of what God's people had to do before Jesus. I am so grateful for each daily reader! It definitely helped me stay on track. Thank you, Summer, for inviting us on this incredible journey!!" ~Naomi Glick, PA

"I have learned so much about God, and what He wants from us. I feel like I'm learning everyday who He is, and how much He loves us. It truly feels like I am gaining a deeper relationship with him. It's all wisdom!" ~Marissa Cooper, TX

"I have read through the Bible twice, but I did it on my own. Having 6,000 women doing it with me has been wonderful. God has blessed me with several women who are encouraging me to step out in faith and share prayer requests more instead of bottling everything up. I am praying a lot more and crying out to God." ~Fran Toal, United Kingdom

"I have always struggled with being consistent in reading God's Word. And to be honest, at the beginning, I struggled to keep up. I did a lot of praying those first few weeks. But since getting on track, this truly has helped me. I feel closer to Jesus. God has taught me through this to love myself and to know I am his daughter. But most importantly, to also listen to Him. Thank you, Summer, for this group. It also has given me over 6,000 new sisters too!" ~Kristy Gannaway, AL

"My life has changed a lot since I started reading the Bible cover to cover. I am at a loss for words, or how to even describe it. I am so proud of myself that I have kept up with the reading. It has opened up my heart. I have more of an understanding of God's Word and a much closer relationship with Him. It's like I am in a whole new world now, and even though there is bad stuff going on in the world, I no longer worry because I know God has got me!" ~Tina Mader, MI

"Reading the Bible cover to cover in a year has kept me accountable. It has been challenging, but very rewarding, to also lead a group of 10 women through it as well. Sometimes the women would get behind, but they would not give up and then would find the time to catch up. I am grateful that they helped keep me accountable, too! This year has pushed me to dig and want to know Him more. Many times, over and over, He has shown up and told me not to fear but to have faith because He will take care of things." ~Edith Schmidt, Canada

A YEAR OF MIRACLES

52 WEEK BIBLE STUDY JOURNAL

A GUIDE TO READING THE BIBLE
COVER TO COVER IN A YEAR

Copyright © 2022 Fear Into Faith Incorporated

All rights reserved. No part of this publication may be reproduced, distributed, or transmitted in any form or by any means, including photocopying, recording, or other electronic methods, without the prior written permission from the publisher, except in the case of brief quotations embodied in critical reviews and certain other noncommercial uses permitted by copyright law. Requests to the publisher for permission should be addressed to the Permissions Department, Kingdom Mindset Publishing, 4621 Reese Rd, Torrance, CA 90505

LIMIT OF LIABILITY/ DISCLAIMER OF WARRANTY: The information in each non-fiction book is intended for use within the United States of America. Each book is meant as a general resource book; it is not meant to provide any legal advice. The Publisher and the Author make no representations or warranties with respect to the accuracy or completeness of the contents of the work and specifically disclaim all warranties of fitness for a particular purpose. The advice and strategies contained therein may not be suitable for every situation. The work is sold with the understanding that the Publisher and the Author are not providing any legal, accounting, or other professional services. If legal, accounting, or other expert assistance is required, the services of competent professionals should be sought. Neither the publisher nor the author shall be liable for damages arising herefrom. The fact that an organization or website is referred to in this work as a citation and/or a potential source of further information does not mean that the author or the publisher endorses the information the organization or website may provide or recommendations it may make. Further, readers should be aware that Internet websites listed in this work may have changed or disappeared between when this work was written and when it is read. The information contained is strictly for educational purposes. Therefore, if you wish to apply ideas contained in this book, or related publications, products, and programs, you are taking full responsibility for your actions. By using this product, you agree that the Publisher and the author cannot be held responsible – directly or indirectly, in full or in part – for any damages or losses that may be suffered as a result of taking action on the information published in this book.

First paperback edition July 2022

Interior Design: Jeremy Holden
Cover Design: Sharon Marta
Editor: Sandi Jenkins & Brit Coppa
ISBN: Print 978-1-7374648-4-6

"Scripture quotations are from The ESV® Bible (The Holy Bible, English Standard Version®), copyright © 2001 by Crossway, a publishing ministry of Good News Publishers. Used by permission. All rights reserved."

Published in the United States of America

Ordering Information:

Quantity sales - Special discounts are available on quantity purchases by churches, corporations, associations, U.S. trade bookstores, wholesalers, and others. For details, contact the publisher at Info@StudyHisWord.com.

For Free Resources and Videos on "How to Use this Bible Study Journal" scan this QR code or go to www.StudyHisWord.com

The author has made every effort to ensure the accuracy of the information within this book was correct and true at the time of publication. The stories printed are the personal accounts of those that submitted them, and not of the author. The author does not assume and hereby disclaims any liability to any party for any loss, damage, or disruption caused by errors or omissions, whether such errors or omissions result from accident, negligence, or any other cause.

This book is dedicated to my father and mother for inspiring me to live and love like Christ, and for supporting and encouraging me to reach higher.

Contents

A Note From The Journal Creator	X
Your Journey Begins Here!	XI
What You Will Find In This Journal	XII
What Can God Not Do?	XVI

Week 1	17	Week 19	89	Week 37	161
Week 2	21	Week 20	93	Week 38	165
Week 3	25	Week 21	97	Week 39	169
Week 4	29	Week 22	101	Week 40	173
Week 5	33	Week 23	105	Week 41	177
Week 6	37	Week 24	109	Week 42	181
Week 7	41	Week 25	113	Week 43	185
Week 8	45	Week 26	117	Week 44	189
Week 9	49	Week 27	121	Week 45	193
Week 10	53	Week 28	125	Week 46	197
Week 11	57	Week 29	129	Week 47	201
Week 12	61	Week 30	133	Week 48	205
Week 13	65	Week 31	137	Week 49	209
Week 14	69	Week 32	141	Week 50	213
Week 15	73	Week 33	145	Week 51	217
Week 16	77	Week 34	149	Week 52	221
Week 17	81	Week 35	153		
Week 18	85	Week 36	157		

Walk In His Ways	225
Prayer Log	226
Praise Report	228
Future Books	232
More From Kingdom Mindset Publishing	233
Free Gift	235
About The Journal Creator	236
Pastoral & Biblical Advisor	236

A Note from the Journal Creator

In April 2020, I finished reading the Bible cover to cover for the first time. My goal was to finish it in one year, it took me two. When I finished, I felt God telling me to do it again and this time to hit my goal.

So... I did a Facebook Live to see if anyone would want to read the Bible with me in a year and hold me accountable. I was hoping to find five friends to read with me. Before I finished that Facebook Live, I had more than 20 women wanting to read the Bible with me. To my surprise, those women began to share my video with their friends and by the end of that day we had over 200 women join. Then, in the days to come, it jumped to 1,000, then 2,000, and then 4,000!

On July 13, 2020 we started the "Fear Into Faith 52-Week Bible Challenge" with over 6,700 women. And to be honest with you - I was freaked out! I cried out to God on my bathroom floor and told Him all the reasons why I was not qualified to lead thousands of women through reading the Bible. God was so gentle with me at that moment. He told me that He had made me a "gatherer of people and a natural encourager," and all He wanted was for me to encourage as many women as possible to read His word cover to cover and He would qualify me for all the rest.

I had no idea how to pull something like this off. A friend suggested that I use a women's Bible Study she had been using. It had a weekly reading plan and journal questions - it was perfect! Until it suddenly jumped to Matthew. Oh no! Women were now confused. "Do we jump ahead to the New Testament now?" "What do we do?" they asked. God was very clear to me that He wanted us to read the Bible cover to cover, like we read every other book, and to not jump around. I told the women that we would no longer use that guide and we would find something else. We searched high and low and could not find a Bible study that went through the Bible cover to cover. It didn't exist!

So, we created it.

Here we are, two years later, with our third Bible Study Journal in your hands. We have men and children doing this Bible study now, and we also have a much bigger vision from God than we ever imagined! Our mission now is to lead one million, church-going Christians to read the Bible cover to cover in a year. And...crazily enough...I am no longer freaked out!

I have seen incredible fruits in my own life from being in God's Word each and every day, and from truly surrendering my life to Him. I want to see God's people be fierce for His Kingdom. And that happens through prayer and reading His Word. Reading God's Word from Genesis to Revelations changed my life. I know it will change yours. I will be praying for you to stick with it and finish, my friend. I promise you it's worth it!

Blessings,

Summer Dey

Your Journey Begins Here!

What materials do you need:
- ☐ This journal
- ☐ Any version or translation of the Bible you would like to use
- ☐ A pen
- ☐ Bible highlighters

We recommend you do not use regular highlighters on your Bible as they can bleed through and destroy pages.

How to use this guide:

Here are some tips to help you use this guide and to succeed in your journey:

- ➛ **Begin when you want.** You can start this journal whenever it works best for you. We will be launching our yearly Bible Challenge on September 19, 2022. If you'd like to join others from around the world and read along with them then you will want to start then.

- ➛ **Find a friend to read with you or lead a group.** There is nothing like accountability to help you achieve your goals. Using this guide and reading the Bible with a friend or a group of people will dramatically increase your chances of finishing reading the Bible in the next year. Plus, you'll play a role in helping others to strengthen their relationship with the Lord as well.

- ➛ **Give yourself grace.** Nearly everyone falls behind at some point. The trick is to catch back up as soon as you can and not give up. If you get too far behind you can choose to jump to where you should be in the reading schedule and catch up later when you can.

STOP RIGHT NOW AND SAVE THE DATE!
September 16-17, 2023, Location TBD.

END OF THE YEAR CELEBRATION - We want to celebrate with you when you finish reading the bible cover to cover. What a HUGE accomplishment! In 2023, we will celebrate on September 16-17th.. During this live event we will get the opportunity to finish reading the last few chapters of the book of Revelation out loud together. It is going to be powerful! We would love to have you there! SAVE THE DATES now and plan to join us either live and in-person or virtually online.

What You Will Find In This Journal

Reading Plan

Each week starts with a **Reading Plan** that lets you read the Bible cover to cover in 52-weeks by reading just 15-20 minutes a day, six days a week. The seventh day is listed as **Rest Day/Catch Up.** This gives you a chance to take the day off from reading or catch up on any reading you may have missed that week.

Faith in Action

This section has a weekly challenge designed to activate your faith and to take things to a deeper level with the Lord.

Journal Questions

Four weekly questions to take what you are reading and connect it on a more personal level.

Reflection & Notes

Use this section each week to make note of any questions you had while reading or anything that stands out to you that needs further reflection.

Gratitude

Use this section to focus on what you are grateful for. What you feed will flourish. When you spend time in gratitude you are shining a light on darkness and it cannot stay. Spend more time in gratitude this year and watch how God shows up!

In the back of the book you will find a **Prayer Log** to track your prayers and see how God answers them.

There is also a **Praise Report** to write down the blessings that God brings into your life.

XIII

Letters To God

In this section you are encouraged to write a letter to God, then spend some time listening to hear back from Him. There are three steps to this process:

Step 1: On the top section of the page you will write a letter to God and share with Him how you are feeling. This is your opportunity to pour your heart out to Him, make requests of Him, ask for guidance on things you are struggling with, etc. Don't overthink it. Just set a 5 minute timer and go for it.

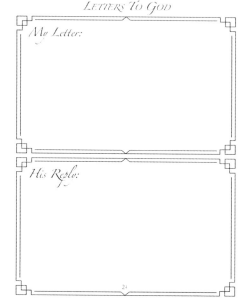

Step 2: Take your Bible and randomly open it and read the first scripture that captures your attention. Make a note of what scripture it is on that page of this journal.

Step 3: Write back whatever message you feel God may be trying to reveal to you through the scripture you just read. Don't waste your time wondering if it is from God or if it is just your own thoughts. Just write whatever comes up for you.

****If you read the random scripture and it doesn't seem to fit what you wrote in your letter then open up your Bible to a different scripture. Do this up to three times. If no scriptures speak to you then just write whatever comes up for you.

Tip: Do not allow yourself to sit in judgment. Just write and see how God shows up for you!

Please watch the video tutorial on how to write your Letter To God:
www.StudyHisWord.com

We Want You to Succeed!

Visit our website **www.StudyHisWord.com** and check out the free videos and resources to go with this journal.

- Tips on how to highlight your Bible
- Details on how to use each section of this journal
- Frequently asked questions
- How to choose the version of the Bible that's right for you
- And more!

JOIN OUR COMMUNITY AND EXPERIENCE READING THE BIBLE WITH OTHERS FROM AROUND THE GLOBE!

Your success is important to us! We want to support you with your goal of reading the Bible cover to cover in a year. By purchasing this study guide you have joined people from around the globe, committed to reading God's Word cover to cover in a year, spending more time with Him than ever before, and supporting others to do so as well.

Join us at www.StudyHisWord.com

Here's what you get:

- **Live Readings** - The daily Bible reading assignments are read live each morning on our YouTube Channel so that those who want to can follow along. Many choose to listen in the morning while driving to work.
- **App** - An app to put the daily readings right into the palm of your hand. It's a great tool to track your progress.
- **Email List** - Subscribe to our email list to hear about new book releases, tools, and upcoming resources.
- **Community** - We will be launching our yearly Bible Challenge on September 19, 2022 with people from all over the world. If you join us after that date, you can hop in and jump to whatever chapter we are in. We will be happy to have you! Check out our website for more details.

You're bringing freedom to others

Your purchase of this journal supports our mission to set captives free. For every journal purchased, we will put a Bible in the hands of someone who has never heard the name of Jesus before. Proceeds also go to support organizations that rescue women and children out of human trafficking.

What Can God Not Do?

Before you begin this year-long journey...

Imagine for a second what your life will look like a year from now when you have finished reading the Bible cover to cover.

What will your life look like when you have spent that much time with God?

How will it affect you?

How will it affect those around you?

Write out how you visualize your life will be when you finish this incredible goal.

The vision I have for my life in a year:

I envision a closer and continually growing relationship with God that is evident in my words and actions.

Week 1

"And he believed in the Lord, and he counted it to him as righteousness." ~*Genesis 15:6*

READING PLAN

Day 1:	Genesis 1-4
Day 2:	Genesis 5-8
Day 3:	Genesis 9-12
Day 4:	Genesis 13-15
Day 5:	Genesis 16-18
Day 6:	Genesis 19-21
Day 7:	Rest Day/Catch Up

Faith in Action

Focus on positive language and how you are speaking toward others and yourself.

Week 1   Date: 9/19 - 9/26 2022

Journal Questions

1. After six days of creation, God rested on the seventh day. He did not have to rest. He's God. He did it as an example to us. Are you following his example and resting? Why, or why not?

   I am following His example because the rest allows me to relax and recharge so that I have stamina for the other 6 days.

2. The Enemy deceived Eve with a small lie. He twisted the truth with "Did God really say?" He knew Eve wouldn't physically die, but she would spiritually die in sin. How can we combat an enemy who also knows scripture? How has the Enemy tried to defeat you with those words, "Did God really say?"

   We can pray for God's clarity. because the enemy tries to defeat us with confusion and misunderstanding.

3. Abraham gave the Melchizedek priest a 10th of all he had - symbolic of a tithe. What is God perhaps asking you to give in faith versus giving out of obligation? Are you being obedient, or clenching with a tight fist?

4. Abraham was recognized as being righteous by faith (Genesis 15:6), and then God gave him the covenant of circumcision, a physical sign. He was righteous first, and then was asked to do something in obedience. What does this speak to you?

Week 1
Reflection & Notes

Gratitude

Thank you, Lord, for the safety and security of our home and family.

Inspiration

I have always believed I am a powerful woman of God. He has given me great influence in the lives of those around me. The Lord has filled me with His power to accomplish great things. Here's the story of the one time He used me to miraculously heal someone.

I attended a weekly single moms' fellowship group. We called our group "Overcomers" and met to bare one another's burdens and pray over each other. We bore our souls without shame as we cried, got angry, comforted, and encouraged each other. This was an environment free of judgment and condemnation. The Lord, through our sisters, ministered to us truth, comfort, strength, hope, joy, life, healing, courage, and faith!

One night, we arrived late and I came in quietly. A few minutes later, another one of our members came in late with a new lady none of us knew. As this new mama walked past me, the Holy Spirit spoke to my spirit and said, "Get up. Anoint her stomach and pray for healing." I would love to tell you I immediately obeyed, but I did not. I sat there and debated with the God of all creation. Have you ever done that? Well, it doesn't work! The Holy Spirit burned inside of me for the duration of our fellowship time. The Lord had healing to impart and He wasn't going to let my momentary lack of faith stop that.

Fellowship ended and we began to pray. The new mama spoke up and asked for prayer to heal her terminal cancer in her stomach. I immediately told her what God had said to me the moment she entered the room and I asked permission to anoint her stomach and pray over her. She informed us all she did not believe in God, but she was out of options and the doctors gave her only weeks to live. Another woman felt led by the Holy Spirit to anoint her head and pray, so I pulled frankincense oil from my purse and together we anointed her head and stomach. We prayed in faith for healing, salvation and peace of mind as we let the Holy Spirit minister through us. The next week, this lady reported back to us that her cancer was completely gone and she had been healed! She declared she now believed in the God who healed her and she planned to go to church that week. Hallelujah!

Just two weeks later, this newly saved mama died in a tragic fire. I learned that day, through many tears, the eternal importance of obeying the Holy Spirit's leading, no matter what! A person's eternal salvation may be on the other side of your absolute obedience to minister to them. You are a powerful person too! The power of the Holy Spirit dwells inside of you. You are capable of doing exceedingly, abundantly above all you can ask, think or imagine! You have miracles inside of you waiting to be released in the name of Jesus, if you will have the faith to believe and the courage to act on that belief.

~Maya Baker

"But the Lord said to Moses, 'Do not fear him, for I have given him into your hand, and all his people, and his land.'" ~Numbers 21:34

Week 2

"And in your offspring shall all the nations of the earth be blessed, because you have obeyed my voice." ~*Genesis 22:18*

READING PLAN

Day 1:   Genesis 22-25
Day 2:   Genesis 26-29
Day 3:   Genesis 30-33
Day 4:   Genesis 34-36
Day 5:   Genesis 37-41
Day 6:   Genesis 42-46
Day 7:   Rest Day/Catch Up

Faith in Action

Write out three goals you would like to accomplish over the next year. Be as specific as you can.

Week 2　　　Date: _____

Journal Questions

1. God asked Abraham to offer his son, Isaac, as a sacrifice. Abraham obeyed and walked in faith even though God had promised him descendants through Isaac. How can this encourage you in your faith?

2. Esau gave up his birthright for food. His flesh overtook him and he was willing to give up his inheritance. Our inheritance is eternal. Is there hidden sin in your life, or areas you are giving in to the flesh, that can rob you of your inheritance? Are you ready to give them up?

3. Jacob wrestled with God and walked away with a limp. This limp was a physical reminder of humility before God. Are there things in your life that God has used to keep you walking in humility before Him? Pray about this.

4. Joseph was sold into slavery by his own family. After many years God prospered him and placed him in position to bless this same family. What lesson can you personally take from this?

Week 2
Reflection & Notes

Gratitude

Letters To God

My Letter:

His Reply:

Week 3

"The Lord is my strength and my song, and He has become my salvation; this is my God, and I will praise Him, my father's God, and I will exalt Him." ~*Exodus 15:2*

READING PLAN

Day 1:	Genesis 47-50
Day 2:	Exodus 1-3
Day 3:	Exodus 4-7
Day 4:	Exodus 8-11
Day 5:	Exodus 12-15
Day 6:	Exodus 16-18
Day 7:	Rest Day/Catch Up

Faith in Action

Write down three things each day that you are grateful for.

Week 3   Date: _____

Journal Questions

1. God heard the groaning of His people. Look up the several Hebrew words for "groan" and "cry" in Exodus 2:23-25, to gain a deeper understanding of what this means. Write what you find below. Just like a parent knows their child's cry - God knows yours. Will you trust Him?

2. List the 10 plagues that God brought on Egypt. Do you know what these 10 plagues represented and why they were significant?

3. The blood on the doorpost from the Passover lamb was how the Israelites were saved. This was prophetic of Christ as our Passover lamb. What is the significance of applying it to the doorpost? How does this relate to our lives today?

4. God led the Israelites with a cloud by day and fire by night. What might this be symbolic of?

Week 3
Reflection & Notes

Gratitude

Inspiration

In 2010, I had an asthma attack that landed me in the emergency room and changed my whole life, leaving me wheelchair dependent. I spent the next few days in the hospital, having tremors and a high heart rate. When I tried to stand up my legs flailed, my back arched, and my body shook as though having a seizure. I had no control. The fear was overwhelming.

That was the start of complete dependency on others. I was unable to eat, dress, wash or brush my hair, or push my own wheelchair. Although frustrated by my circumstances, I managed to retain my sense of humor and faith, truly expecting the symptoms would leave as fast as they had come on. But, I was wrong. My symptoms only grew steadily worse, and brought about extreme life changes. The unsightly spasms and painful contortions of my body had most friends avoiding the uncomfortable sight. Only a few faithfull stuck around to.

My lack of motor skills and arms spasms made an electric chair a safety hazard. I had to be fitted for a customized wheelchair with a harness to stop me from falling out. It even had wrist guards to keep my hands straight. I even had to have all my teeth removed due to cracking and chipping from all the spasms, which also led to infection. The extreme pain called for heavy painkillers and I was put on Fentanyl patches for nine years. All this led to an anguishing, senseless time where I could no longer control emotions or express feelings in appropriate ways. I was clouded in a daze from all the medication and didn't notice the years as they passed.

Before I knew it, eleven years had gone by and I was still unable to stop my body from flying in all directions, despite weekly therapy from dedicated, yet defeated physical therapists. I was now on twenty three daily medications, and was spasming all the time, even when I slept. The doctors felt hopeless about my situation. When my Neurologist finally spoke the words to me, "You will never walk again," it left me feeling crushed and my husband feeling completely helpless. I had days of despair, anger, and defeat. However, those days never lasted very long because I knew my God. Sometimes it felt like He was my only friend. He also gave me joy and encouragement.

Two months after I that doctor visit, I was watching a church service online for Open Door Church in Dallas, Texas, and the Holy Spirit moved! I joyfully went to run a bath, turned on the water and reached back for my wheelchair. At that moment, I became annoyed that I couldn't reach it, thinking to myself, "I must have left the brakes off," and it had rolled away. I looked over my shoulder. It was not there! I found myself wandering back to my bed and there sat my wheelchair waiting for me. I had walked to the bathroom without realizing it. I immediately raced down the hall calling out my husband's name. I will never forget the look on his face when he saw me and quickly told me, "Be careful!" The look on my husband's face was priceless but it was nothing compared to the look on my doctor's face when I got up and walked around the room during my next visit. He couldn't believe his eyes, and neither could the rest of his staff, when I walked right out of his office!

I have been walking ever since! No more asthma attacks, spasms or tremors, simply walking like everyone else. Healed by my Mighty King Jesus to live in abundant joy! I am grateful for the experiences He walked me through because I am a walking miracle who now gets to inspire people with my testimony that Jesus still heals!

~Nikki Cruise

Week 4

"You are to speak to the people of Israel and say, 'Above all you shall keep My Sabbaths, for this is a sign between Me and you throughout your generations, that you may know that I, the Lord, sanctify you.'" ~*Exodus 31:13*

READING PLAN

Day 1:	Exodus 19-21
Day 2:	Exodus 22-25
Day 3:	Exodus 26-29
Day 4:	Exodus 30-32
Day 5:	Exodus 33-36
Day 6:	Exodus 37-40
Day 7:	Rest Day/Catch Up

Faith in Action

Pray for someone who you know is going through a difficult season.

Week 4 Date: _____

Journal Questions

1. God brought the children of Israel out of bondage and then gave them the Commandments to obey. This is a picture of grace, and how we don't have to do anything but simply believe Him for our salvation. What can we learn from this regarding our own salvation and obedience?

2. The altar they made was of bronze. When the people pushed their sacrifice up on the altar they could likely see their reflection in the altar. How powerful is that? What do you think was the purpose of seeing their own reflection while lifting their animal up to be slain?

3. In Exodus 32, God threatens to destroy the people because of their disobedience. Then, in a marvelous picture of intercession, Moses prays for mercy rather than judgment, and God relents. Are there situations or people in your life where God may be calling you to intercede and ask for mercy?

4. In Exodus 36, God gave Bezalel and Oholiab wisdom to do all the work that God asked of Moses and the people. God had an assignment, and then provided people and wisdom to have the job done well. Meditate on this. What does this mean to you?

Week 4
Reflection & Notes

Gratitude

Letters To God

My Letter:

His Reply:

Week 5

"Speak to all the congregation of the people of Israel and say to them, 'You shall be holy, for I the Lord your God am holy.'"
~*Leviticus 19:2*

READING PLAN

Day 1:	Leviticus 1-4
Day 2:	Leviticus 5-8
Day 3:	Leviticus 9-12
Day 4:	Leviticus 13-15
Day 5:	Leviticus 16-19
Day 6:	Leviticus 20-23
Day 7:	Rest Day/Catch Up

Faith in Action

Ask yourself if there's anything that may be hindering your relationship with God. Make a list of those things, then take some time and pray a prayer of repentance, asking God to forgive you.

Week 5   Date: _____

Journal Questions

1. In Leviticus 10, Aaron's two sons brought "strange" fire before God. What does that word "strange" mean in Hebrew? What does this account show or teach us?

2. Leviticus 17:11 says, "Blood makes atonement for life." Why was the blood being shed so important in the sacrifice? Reflect on how this speaks prophetically of our salvation.

3. Leviticus has a theme of "clean" versus "unclean." Clean in Hebrew means "pure." Unclean means "impure." What could this mean for how we are to live for and worship God?

4. Look at the Lord's feasts mentioned in Leviticus 23. Consider the significance of each one of these and what they are pointing towards?

Week 5
Reflection & Notes

Gratitude

Inspiration

The family was so excited! It was September, 1990, and we were going to have our ultrasound to find out the gender of the first baby on both sides of the family. It wasn't long before we were called back to the ultrasound room. The technician wasn't very chatty, and she didn't even ask us if we wanted to know the baby's gender. She excused herself and came back with the doctor I was scheduled to see that day. He looked somber and said, "I hate to have to give you bad news, but your baby has a choroid plexus cyst. The outcome won't be good. I recommend terminating the pregnancy." The happiest day of our lives took a nosedive.

When I could finally speak, I told the doctor my baby was going to be fine. God was going to heal my baby. Although I had two questions for him. I wanted to know if we were going to have a girl or a boy, and what was a choroid plexus cyst? We were expecting a girl, and a choroid plexus cyst was a cyst that forms in the choroid plexus area of the brain. I worked at one of the largest facilities for the developmentally disabled and special needs population in the South, so knowing what kind of cyst this was interested me. That way I could give all the glory to God for this coming miracle.

The enemy tried to make me afraid, but the love I had for my baby, not to mention my faith in God as my Jehovah Rapha, wouldn't allow me to succumb to fear. After telling us how bad the situation was, the doctor agreed to do a repeat ultrasound in one month. If the cyst had not shrunk or had grown, the pregnancy would be terminated according to him. I told him we'd see him in a month, but God would heal my baby girl!

We got home, and I had my mother and mother-in-law start a prayer chain at their churches. I asked every Christian I knew to pray. God had given me peace that surpassed all understanding. A week before the repeat ultrasound, it happened! I was at a stop sign having just left work, singing the old hymn, "Living By Faith," and knew at that exact moment my baby's brain was healed. It felt as if someone reached into my belly and plucked the cyst out. Well, He did! I couldn't wait to get home to call and tell everyone my news!

The next doctor's appointment finally came. I walked in grinning from ear to ear. I told the ultrasound technician she wouldn't find a cyst because it was gone. She nodded politely. Halfway through the exam, she excused herself. My husband grabbed my hand, not knowing what to think. This time, she came back with several doctors and nurses. The room began to fill up with on-lookers. Many of them were crying. The doctor who suggested terminating my pregnancy told us the cyst was gone. The surrounding brain tissue must have absorbed it. I told him, "Yes, it's gone, but God took it. I felt it when He did." At that, even he had tears glistening in his eyes.

At 6:19 am, on April 18, 1991, my daughter, Blair, was born. She was beautiful and very alert. She still is.

Psalm 139:13-14 states, "For You created my inmost being; You knitted me together in my mother's womb. I praise You because I am fearfully and wonderfully made; Your works are wonderful; I know full well." He is a wonder working God!

~Jamie Gatchell

Week 6

"The Lord bless you and keep you; the Lord make His face shine upon you and be gracious to you; the Lord lift up His countenance upon you and give you peace. 'So shall they put my name upon the people of Israel, and I will bless them.'" ~*Numbers 6:24-27*

READING PLAN

Day 1:	Leviticus 24-27
Day 2:	Numbers 1-3
Day 3:	Numbers 4-6
Day 4:	Numbers 7-9
Day 5:	Numbers 10-13
Day 6:	Numbers 14-16
Day 7:	Rest Day/Catch Up

Faith in Action

Make every effort to pronounce the blessing of the Lord over your children or other loved ones this week.

Week 6　　　Date: _____

Journal Questions

1. In Numbers 6, we learn of the Nazarite vow. What are the three elements of the vow and how might they be significant to our lives today?

2. Out of the ten spies that went to spy out the land, only two came back with a good report? What did they choose to see versus what the others chose to see? Reflect on challenging areas in your own life. Are you seeing through the eyes of the ten, or the two?

3. The priestly blessing (Numbers 6) is a powerful prayer. It's a great prayer to say over people. How could you implement this prayer into your daily or weekly routine?

4. In Numbers 11:1, the people complain incurring God's anger. Another version says "it was evil in the ears of God." What is at the heart of complaining and why does God see it as evil? Are there areas you tend to complain about? What does complaining create in your life?

Week 6

Reflection & Notes

Gratitude

Letters To God

My Letter:

His Reply:

Week 7

"God is not man, that He should lie, or a son of man, that He should change His mind. Has He said, and will He not do it? Or has He spoken, and will He not fulfill it?" ~*Numbers 23:19*

READING PLAN

Day 1:	Numbers 17-19
Day 2:	Numbers 20-22
Day 3:	Numbers 23-26
Day 4:	Numbers 27-30
Day 5:	Numbers 31-33
Day 6:	Numbers 34-36
Day 7:	Rest Day/Catch Up

Faith in Action

Repeat this prayer ~ "Dear Lord, help me submit to the process of delay. Help me wait patiently and trust that Your plans for me are perfect and just what I need at this time. Father, I pray for wisdom while on this journey. Help me to not look right or left, but keep my focus on You, the author and finisher of my faith. Amen."

Week 7   Date: _____

Journal Questions

1. God asked the people to not sacrifice an unclean beast to Him. What is an unclean beast? (Leviticus 11) Why would He say that to them? What could it represent?

2. In Numbers 21, we hear of the story of the bronze serpent. This symbol is often used in our medical community even today. Reflect on the elements of the story and how they point to the Cross. What was required for the people to be saved?

3. Many people died in the wilderness because of disobedience to God and His commands. How can this be an example for you and how can you apply it to your life today?

4. In Numbers 23, Balak wanted to curse the Israelites so he called Balaam to come and curse them, but he couldn't do it. Whenever he tried, God would not allow him to curse His chosen people. As a person who believes upon Jesus, you are grafted into His chosen people. Does this encourage you? How can you apply this truth to your walk?

Week 7
Reflection & Notes

Gratitude

Inspiration

I had a dream one night that would change my life forever. In the dream, I was dialing 911. When I woke up from the dream, I sprang up because I felt like I had been struck in my chest. I could barely breathe because pain was shooting down my left arm and into my elbow. I was sweating profusely as my heart rate slowed dramatically. I felt disoriented as I stumbled into the living room to pick up the phone and dial 911. My breathing was so shallow I could barely speak. I knew I was dying.

I was drifting in and out of consciousness when the paramedics finally got to me. They put me on a stretcher and that was the last thing I remember before falling into a coma. They contacted my parents, who were four and a half hours away. Everything went from bad to worse. I went into respiratory arrest which caused cardiac arrest. The paramedics worked hard to get me stabilized. While still in the ambulance, I died and they brought me back. They put a tube down my throat to put me on a respirator, which caused me to aspirate and gave me pneumonia in my lung. When they put the IV in, the saline began to leak into the surrounding tissue which created a black, third degree burn. They wrapped it with a bandage.

Dave and Joyce Meyer were my first visitors after waking from the coma. They prayed for me. As they were praying, the doctor issued local anesthesia to deaden an area on my left upper thigh to do a skin graft. They could not put me back to sleep in the condition my body was in. Once my body could handle it, they put me back into a coma. While in the coma, my lung collapsed. This time, they brought my parents in and told them to say their goodbyes.

My parents started a prayer chain through Joyce Meyer Ministries and the distribution department I worked in. As they were praying, they saw three angels enter my hospital room. The third angel stood right in front of where I was laying down. That angel breathed on me with the breath of life. The breath of life filled my lungs and bronchial tubes. From that point on, everything turned around.

I had about thirteen different bags of medicine going through my IV. I was on a ventilator for twelve days. Then they transferred me to the ICU for sixteen days. After that, they placed me in a private room for another week to gain strength to leave the hospital. I was in the hospital a total of twenty-three days. The Lord laid Psalms 23 on my heart to meditate on for the rest of that year.

It has been almost 22 years since then and I am fully recovered from that experience.

By the way, I saw Heaven! While my spirit was out of my body, I saw the paramedics working on me to get me back. Heaven is so beautiful and words cannot really describe what I saw! I saw a garden and it had flower combinations and colors we do not see here on earth. I could walk without destroying the flowers. The peace was otherworldly. Everything was so easy and felt like I was moving without effort. I was also taken into a huge large field of wheat. While there, I saw different scenes from my life: when I was a toddler, a young girl, and throughout my elementary years. These were different moments in my life where I would be outside in my yard, lifting my hands, laughing and singing songs to Jesus, but the difference was now Jesus was there doing this with me. Heaven is real!

~*Stacy McLain*

Week 8

"You shall love the Lord your God with all your heart and with all your soul and with all your might." ~*Deuteronomy 6:5*

READING PLAN

Day 1:	Deuteronomy 1-4
Day 2:	Deuteronomy 5-8
Day 3:	Deuteronomy 9-11
Day 4:	Deuteronomy 12-15
Day 5:	Deuteronomy 16-18
Day 6:	Deuteronomy 19-21
Day 7:	Rest Day/Catch Up

Faith in Action

Do you believe you're going through a transition, big or small? List steps you can take to be successful in this season. Make a timeline to help you meet your goals.

Week 8 Date: _____

Journal Questions

1. Lot and Esau received their portion before Israel entered into their promised land. Instead, Israel stayed in the wilderness for 40 years before "receiving their portion." Sometimes it looks like others are receiving their blessings first. Does that mean God has forgotten you? Or is He perhaps preparing you for what's to come?

2. What is the point of the "wilderness?" The Isralites wandered for 40 years in the wilderness. What does God say through Moses about this in Deuteronomy 8?

3. How do we recognize a false prophet according to Deuteronomy 13?

4. "Do not learn according to the abominations of the nations" is repeated over and over in Scripture. What does that mean? What is an abomination? Are we to worship God as other nations worshiped their gods?

Week 8
Reflection & Notes

Gratitude

Letters To God

My Letter:

His Reply:

Week 9

"Have I not commanded you? Be strong and courageous. Do not be frightened, and do not be dismayed, for the Lord your God is with you wherever you go." ~*Joshua 1:9*

READING PLAN

Day 1:	Deuteronomy 22-25
Day 2:	Deuteronomy 26-28
Day 3:	Deuteronomy 29-31
Day 4:	Deuteronomy 32-34
Day 5:	Joshua 1-4
Day 6:	Joshua 5-8
Day 7:	Rest Day/Catch Up

Faith in Action

Take time to be with the Lord in nature: go for a walk, hike, swim, etc. Focus on being grateful for this beautiful world around you and soak in the presence of your Heavenly Father.

Week 9 Date: _____

Journal Questions

1. God tells us not to mix or sow seed together, or wear different fabrics (specifically wool and linen) together? Why? What do you think "pure" worship looks like for us today?

2. In Deuteronomy 27-28, God gives us the blessings and the curses. They are if-then statements. Read through them, reflecting on their relevance for our lives today.

3. Following God's good, set-apart instruction, is not too hard for us (Deuteronomy 30:11). Have you felt at times that His instruction is hard or burdensome? Why do you think this is? How can these verses help us in walking out His commands?

4. In the beginning of the book of Joshua (1:7-8), God spoke to Joshua. He commanded the people to meditate on the Torah day and night. What is the Torah? How should we apply this to our lives today?

Week 9
Reflection & Notes

Gratitude

Inspiration

I was making my way home from a routine business trip. While driving down the highway, I suddenly dropped my soda cap and unbuckled my seat belt to reach down on the floor to grab it. When I finally looked up, I realized I was crossing the center line and was dangerously close to hitting a Chevy Suburban. I immediately over-corrected and the resulting strain on my Escalade caused the driver's side rear axle to break and the tire came off. My car careened into a ditch, where it stood upright, spinning like a top on its front end. I hit the ceiling and was knocked unconscious.

According to eye witness accounts, my car spun three to four rotations before I was half way ejected through the driver's side window. The Escalade came down to a rest on top of me. I regained consciousness wondering if I was paralyzed and discovered my predicament. I was pinned under the car. I immediately called out the name of Jesus and was able to bench press my way out from under the vehicle. That was my first miracle.

In horrific pain, I steadily called upon Jesus as bystanders tried to console me. When paramedics arrived, they determined my injuries were too extensive to transport me by ambulance. An air transport was ordered. I was awake and alert so the chaplain came to me and asked if he could notify anyone. I told him to call my brother, and a pastor friend in Dallas, Texas. My pastor friend held intercessory prayer during his service for me, and my brother called his church to do the same. My brother also called my parents who went to church that night and they too interceded on my behalf.

I had sustained a lot of injuries. Among them, I had crushed my ribs, front and back, and my liver and my intestines were also damaged. As I was prepared for emergency surgery, people prayed for me and I diligently continued to call on Jesus. Twenty hours later, I walked out of the hospital without surgery and without a single debilitating injury. That was my second miracle.

God proved His goodness in extraordinary ways! On that less than routine business trip, I had purchased reclaimed, precious metals from scrap catalytic converters that sat in scrap yards. The night I crashed my Escalade, I had thirty thousand dollars with me that landed on the highway. A prison work crew on that stretch of roadway found it, gave it to a fireman who turned it over to the police. A DEA agent was promptly sent to the hospital to question me. They suspected I was a drug dealer due to the flashy car and thirty thousand dollars in cash. I quickly proved I was a legitimate scrap metal dealer and they swiftly returned my money. That was my third miracle. God Is generous with His mercies.

The accident took away my selfish focus of becoming the world's strongest man and turned my focus to God. Since that day, I have never wanted to compete in lifting events, even though I still lift and I am very strong. God clearly had other plans. Instead of competing, I ended up going to Romania for missionary work and wound up marrying my interpreter. God is so good, and the power of prayer coupled with faith is real and powerful.

~Jayme Berube

Week 10

"But as for me and my house, we will serve the Lord." ~*Joshua 24:15*

READING PLAN

Day 1:	Joshua 9-12
Day 2:	Joshua 13-16
Day 3:	Joshua 17-20
Day 4:	Joshua 21-24
Day 5:	Judges 1-3
Day 6:	Judges 4-6
Day 7:	Rest Day/Catch Up

Faith in Action

Be kind. Kindness always wins. Do three random acts of kindness this week.

Week 10   Date: _____

Journal Questions

1. Why did God tell Joshua and the Israelites to put everyone from the nations "under the ban?" What do you think this represents?

2. Read Joshua's command to Israel in chapter 23 as if he is saying it to you. What is He commanding you today?

3. God was trying the Israelites to see if they would follow His ways. (Judges 2) God will test us to see if we will stand up for Him and His Ways. Sometimes we are quick to blame the Enemy for everything. What if sometimes it is God testing us? Have you been tested at a particular moment in your walk?

4. Sometimes there are things we are asked to do by God, and we know He wants us to do it, but it may not make sense to our human understanding. Are you willing to walk in obedience even if it doesn't make sense? Why or why not? If you hesitate, why? What can you do or choose to implement to fully walk in obedience?

Week 10
Reflection & Notes

Gratitude

Letters To God

My Letter:

His Reply:

Week 11

"At this, she bowed down with her face to the ground. She asked him, 'Why have I found such favor in your eyes that you notice me—a foreigner?'" ~Ruth 2:10

READING PLAN

Day 1:	Judges 7-10
Day 2:	Judges 11-14
Day 3:	Judges 15-17
Day 4:	Judges 18-21
Day 5:	Ruth 1-4
Day 6:	1 Samuel 1-3
Day 7:	Rest Day/Catch Up

Faith in Action

Take some time this week to remember how God has blessed you. Write a list of those blessings.

Week 11 Date: _____

Journal Questions

1. Gideon set up a shoulder garment to gaze upon, and it became a snare. Our flesh so desperately desires to worship a "thing." What things have you elevated in your life that need to come down today?

2. In Judges 16, Delilah asks Samson three times for the source of his strength. After the first two, she unsuccessfully attempts to have him captured. Even after this, he reveals the source of his strength to her! Why do you think this is and what can we learn from it? (Consider especially verse 16:20.)

3. Ruth was a foreigner, and then married Boaz, which grafted her into his family. Jesus was in the lineage of Boaz. Why is this important and what insights can we gather from it as believers today?

4. Even just a few generations after the Exodus, the Israelites quickly forgot all that God had done to bless them. What about in our generation, and our own life? Why do you think it is so easy to forget all that He has done?

Week 11
Reflection & Notes

Gratitude

Inspiration

Mike had congestive heart failure and was at the point of death. His doctor told him that a heart transplant would give him his only chance to live. However, he was too ill to survive the surgery. He was put into hospice care and sent home to die.

The Sunday after he was sent home, he was brought to church for prayer. The entire congregation gathered around Mike to pray for him. As we prayed, I heard that still, small voice of the Lord asking me, "Why are you praying for him to be healed? What he needs is a new heart!" I had prayed for hundreds of people to receive a new spiritual heart through water baptism, but never had I prayed for a new physical organ.

I moved to lay hands on Mike and pray for him to receive a new heart. Before I could make it to the front, my young friend Peter, came up and laid hands on Mike's back. I put my hands on Mike's shoulders and Peter began to pray for Mike to receive a new heart!

Peter's prayer for Mike was itself a miracle. Until recently, Peter suffered from an extreme form of autism that caused him to be extremely withdrawn from people. In the years I had known him, I had not heard him string more than two or three words together in a single sentence. At a recent Sunday morning service, Peter surprised everyone when he grabbed the microphone during worship. He gave a long and detailed testimony of how the Lord healed him. Not even his mother knew that healing had occurred before he gave his testimony. God's glory was compounded as we watched Peter pray for Mike Reel without hesitation.

Mike Reel was supposedly in bed awaiting death. But, Mike didn't die. He started feeling better, so much that when his family was not watching, he snuck out to the garage and put a new engine in his Subaru.

Six months after he was sent home to die, Stanford Hospital called to ask for a copy of Mike's death certificate so they could close his case. His wife answered the phone and said, "Why are you talking about a death certificate? I don't know anything about that. Here, maybe you should talk to Mike," and handed him the phone. Medical staff asked Mike to come in right away so they could evaluate him.

Stanford physicians conducted a battery of tests and scans. The cardiac surgeon treating Mike entered the exam room with his chart extremely upset. He yelled at the technician for mixing up the patients' charts. He demanded to see Mike Reel's correct scans. The technician looked at Mike's wristband and identified the patient as Mike Reel, listing the proper ID number, and then returned to the charts the doctor held. They identified that it was indeed the chart belonging to Mike Reel.

The stunned cardiologist retreated back to his office and a few moments later returned with half a dozen other cardiologists and the head of the department. He examined Mike and exclaimed, "You have a new heart! How did you get a new heart? You have no scar! What surgeon gave you a heart transplant without a scar?" The missing scar was indeed proof that God had answered our prayers and was the Great Physician who gave Mike Reel a new heart.

Over a decade later, my friend Mike is still with us. He is working as a carpenter and a mechanic, occasionally fixing cars for all of his friends. Once at the brink of death, he now lives his life to the fullest and without limit.

~Dr. Richard Yarbrough

Week 12

"But Samuel replied: 'Does the Lord delight in burnt offerings and sacrifices as much as in obeying the Lord? To obey is better than sacrifice, and to heed is better than the fat of rams.'"
~1 Samuel 15:22

READING PLAN

Day 1:	1 Samuel 4-7
Day 2:	1 Samuel 8-11
Day 3:	1 Samuel 12-14
Day 4:	1 Samuel 15-17
Day 5:	1 Samuel 18-21
Day 6:	1 Samuel 22-25
Day 7:	Rest Day/Catch Up

Faith in Action

Take some time this week to look at what is contributing to any stress in your life. What action steps will you take to move forward with less stress?

Week 12   Date: _____

Journal Questions

1. Hannah was a strong woman of faith. God gave her a son. He answered her prayer. What is something you are fervently praying for? What can you learn from Hannah's story of faith?

2. When Samuel was young, he didn't recognize God was speaking to him until the third time. Do you know how to recognize God's voice? What can you do to hear Him more?

3. King Saul messed up numerous times. What was the common theme of his transgressions?

4. What can we learn from how David treats Saul in 1 Samuel 24? Are there any "Sauls" in your life that you can apply these lessons to?

Week 12
Reflection & Notes

Gratitude

Letters To God

My Letter:

His Reply:

Week 13

"Be of good courage, and let us be courageous for our people, and for the cities of our God, and may the Lord do what seems good to Him." ~2 Samuel 10:12

READING PLAN

Day 1:	1 Samuel 26-28
Day 2:	1 Samuel 29-31
Day 3:	2 Samuel 1-4
Day 4:	2 Samuel 5-8
Day 5:	2 Samuel 9-12
Day 6:	2 Samuel 13-15
Day 7:	Rest Day/Catch Up

Faith in Action

Pray and ask God to help you trust Him in all you do.

Week 13 Date: _____

Journal Questions

1. Saul used witchcraft to call up Samuel the prophet from the dead because he felt distant from God and wanted a "quick fix" answer. This is deliberately against God's Word. Have you ever desired a "quick fix" answer so badly that you've deliberately disobeyed to get an answer? How did it turn out?

2. King David had the men divide the spoils between those who fought and those who stayed to protect their stuff. Some men were upset that it wasn't fair. What do you think? Have you ever compared your situation to others and felt like it was not fair? How can this story help with those feelings?

3. "Why have you despised the Word of God to do evil in His eyes?" (2 Samuel 12:9) When we choose evil, or go against God's Word, to Him, we are despising His Word. Have you been guilty of this? Confess, repent and know He forgives quickly. How can we protect ourselves from despising His Word?

4. King David was the "apple of God's eye." He was hand-picked by God and would carry the lineage of Jesus. Yet, he sinned and fell short more than once. What do you notice about King David when he fell short and sinned against God? What example does that give us?

Week 13
Reflection & Notes

Gratitude

Inspiration

Years ago, I was diagnosed with anxiety, depression, panic disorder, severe PTSD, and suffered through daily seizures. It was a very miserable time in my life. Through Biblical forgiveness work, I was able to become completely free from all of it for four years. I was convinced it was gone for good.

Then, in 2019, I lost everything. I lost a pregnancy. I lost the company I had built. I lost my childhood dream I'd worked for. I ended up back in severe depression, with PTSD, and seizures again. Just like the first time, I thought it would all go away, but it didn't.

Fifteen months went by quickly. My life shifted. Our family moved fulltime into an RV and began traveling. I had less stress in my life. I was happy and fulfilled, yet I was still suffering from seizures. I finally went to the doctor where they ran countless tests, but didn't find answers. Eventually, a neurologist officially diagnosed me with epilepsy. I was crushed! I had been in denial that anything was wrong with me. Even though having seizures had become so normal that my kids didn't flinch anymore when I had them.

I decided to not be defined by my diagnosis. I had overcome seizures before, and I believed this time God would heal me for His glory. I would tell people, "A doctor diagnosed me with epilepsy, but God is going to heal me. I don't know where, or when, but I know He is!"

Yet, when that day came, I still walked in denial. Even though I had witnessed a friend be miraculously healed out of a wheelchair, somehow a part of me still doubted that miracles were real.

In March of 2022, I was miraculously healed at a business training event. There was a pastor, named Benny Perez, on stage healing people in the crowd. He began saying, "There is somebody here having issues with your brain..." As he spoke, I remember thinking to myself, "That sounds like it could be me," while looking over the crowd and wondering why no one was raising their hand. Then I heard the Holy Spirit whisper, "No one is raising their hand because it's YOU he is talking about!"

At that moment, I screamed in my head, "Noooooooo!" and began to argue with God that it couldn't possibly be me! My body suddenly began to burn like it was on fire, and a force beyond my control began to propel my body to the stage. When I got there, Pastor Benny spoke to me for a minute, and then he declared, "As quickly as it came, it's leaving even quicker now!" And then I fell to the ground...not once...not twice...but three times! As I sat up on the floor, I felt hot, dazed, and confused. Yet... I knew I was healed!

What was also amazing, is that earlier that day, I had posted on Facebook that I was looking for stories of miraculous healing for my next Bible study journal I was creating. I never dreamed God wanted me to be one of those stories!

It has been months now and I have been seizure free, which still is incredible to me. Honestly, I still have moments of doubt about my healing. When someone is healed out of a wheelchair, you can see it. You can see them walk again. I can't show people evidence that I have been healed from seizures. I simply don't have them anymore.

I think that is why God wanted me to share my story with you. To let you know it's okay if you have doubt. Just don't stay there! I almost let doubt steal away my moment of healing. Don't miss your moment. Miracles are everywhere, and I believe God has one waiting for you!

~Summer Dey

Week 14

"And may your hearts be fully committed to the Lord our God, to live by His decrees and obey His commands, as at this time."
~1 Kings 8:61

READING PLAN

Day 1:	2 Samuel 16-18
Day 2:	2 Samuel 19-21
Day 3:	2 Samuel 22-24
Day 4:	1 Kings 1-4
Day 5:	1 Kings 5-7
Day 6:	1 Kings 8-10
Day 7:	Rest Day/Catch Up

Faith in Action

Recount blessings that God has already given you and done in your life. Give Him praise for what He has already done for you, even if you are walking through a season of challenges.

Week 14 Date: _____

Journal Questions

1. King David was faithful to God and His ways. He went through hard times, but David never swayed from his faithfulness to God. When times get challenging what do you tend to do?

2. When building the temple, no hammer or chisel was heard in the temple of God (1 Kings 6:7). They had great reverence toward the set-apart place where He would meet the people. What great reverence and fear of Him they had! What are some ways that you can revere God in a similar way?

3. Read and meditate on King Solomon's prayer in 1 Kings 8. What do you see?

4. There are consequences to sinning against God. What is sin? Look at 1 John 3:4. What is the difference between "sin" and "temptation?" Can they be the same? Why or why not?

Week 14
Reflection & Notes

Gratitude

Letters To God

My Letter:

His Reply:

Week 15

"'Don't be afraid,' the prophet answered. 'Those who are with us are more than those who are with them.'" ~2 Kings 6:16

READING PLAN

Day 1:   1 Kings 11-14
Day 2:   1 Kings 15-18
Day 3:   1 Kings 19-22
Day 4:   2 Kings 1-3
Day 5:   2 Kings 4-7
Day 6:   2 Kings 8-11
Day 7:   Rest Day/Catch Up

Faith in Action

Pray. Pray for God to move through you to spread His gift of grace and mercy to others this week.

Week 15 Date: _____

Journal Questions

1. King Solomon was one of the wisest people to walk the earth and yet he still fell into the lust of the flesh and massive sin. He had hundreds of wives that turned his heart away from the one true God and His ways. How can we succeed where this wise man failed?

2. What can we learn from the faith and trust that the widow had during her encounter with Elijah the prophet in 1 Kings 17?

3. 2 Kings 5 tells us the story of Naaman, commander of the army for Aram, a nation not of Israel. What can we learn about God's heart in this story? Was Naaman an Israelite or a non-believer? Why did he first question what he was told to do to be healed?

4. Elisha prayed and asked God to open his servant's eyes to see the horses and chariots of fire around the army that had encircled them. How does this encourage you? Is there a time when you knew you had protection surrounding you that wasn't visible to the human eye?

Week 15
Reflection & Notes

Gratitude

Inspiration

June 26, 1971, I was taken ill with what they thought was heatstroke. I had been complaining of terrible headaches, had a fever of 106, and was talking out of my mind. Two days later, when my aunt and grandma were visiting, they noticed I was unresponsive. My mom was shocked. She thought I was just sleeping. They immediately rushed me to Saint Francis Hospital. By this point, I was already in a coma. I was thrashing uncontrollably as they tried to work on me. My mom said she began to repeat to me, "Jesus, Jesus, Jesus!" and I calmed down enough for them to do what they needed to.

It was later determined I had Encephalitis and Spinal Meningitis. They sent a priest in to give me my last rights. Doctors told my parents I had less than 8 hours to live, and if by any chance I did live, I would probably be a vegetable for the rest of my life.

For three days straight, I screamed nonstop. I had to be tied completely to the bed from my head to my feet because of the constant thrashing. A nurse had to hold something in my mouth to keep me from swallowing my tongue. My family began to get countless people around the world to pray for a miracle. They were very close friends with Oral Roberts at the time, and he stopped mid-sermon, in front of 3,000 people to pray for me.

Then, as quickly as it started, I suddenly stopped thrashing after three days in a coma. When I woke up, I can remember trying to move. I tried to talk, but couldn't. I kept hearing the beeping noises, and voices calmly repeating my name, "Todd, Todd, Todd, it's alright, Todd, Todd, Todd."

The nurse started hollering for help and people ran in all around the bed. Everyone was talking and everything was white. My mind was racing, thinking it was a dream. I thought to myself, "Am I dead? Where am I? Who are these people?" They checked my vitals, and I kept trying to talk. I remember feeling scared. And I kept hearing those calm voices saying, "Todd, Todd, Todd." When they finally removed the tube out of my mouth, I started talking. They were amazed. They started asking me all kinds of questions. They removed all of my restraints.

At this point, I could see three women at the foot of my bed; two caucasian women with an African American woman in the middle. They were beautiful and were wearing all white. They said, "Todd, Todd, Todd," and then all the other questions started again. They were crazy questions, I thought.

My mom and dad were outside the door to my room putting on what looked like white robes, so I still thought I was still dreaming. It turns out they were putting on sanitary gowns.

After two more spinal taps, numerous tests, countless questions and visits from several more doctors, I was finally released. The doctors told my parents it was a miracle that only God could have done! I had gone from being given less than 8 hours to live, to walking out the door, in just three weeks.

At the time, I was the youngest person to survive with the strains of encephalitis and spinal meningitis that I had. It was especially miraculous that I endured no side effects or complications of any type as well.

Later, when I asked who the three women were at the foot of my bed when I woke up out of a coma, no one could tell me. I never saw them again after that brief encounter. I described them to everyone and none of them saw them, but me. I now know Jesus sent them, and know they were my Guardian Angels.

~Todd Jones

Week 16

"But you shall fear the Lord your God, and He will deliver you out of the hand of all your enemies." ~*2 Kings 17:39*

READING PLAN

Day 1:	2 Kings 12-15
Day 2:	2 Kings 16-18
Day 3:	2 Kings 19-22
Day 4:	2 Kings 23-25
Day 5:	1 Chronicles 1-4
Day 6:	1 Chronicles 5-8
Day 7:	Rest Day/Catch Up

Faith in Action

Smile. You never know who you are influencing.

Week 16 Date: _____

Journal Questions

1. Many times new kings would come in and attempt to change things back to God's ways. However, they rarely took down the "high places" (2 Kings 14:4). What is a high place? How is this relevant in our modern day?

2. What high places are you keeping "up" in your life that you know He's asking you to take down?

3. What was the difference between the kings that did evil in the eyes of God and those that did good? What was evil in the eyes of God?

4. Judah and Israel became two separate nations and both were exiled because of their disobedience. Where were they exiled and for how long? Did they ever come out of exile? (2 Kings 17 & 24)

Week 16
Reflection & Notes

Gratitude

Letters To God

My Letter:

His Reply:

Week 17

"Look to the Lord and His strength; seek His face always."
~1 Chronicles 16:11

READING PLAN

Day 1:   1 Chronicles 9-12
Day 2:   1 Chronicles 13-16
Day 3:   1 Chronicles 17-19
Day 4:   1 Chronicles 20-22
Day 5:   1 Chronicles 23-26
Day 6:   1 Chronicles 27-29
Day 7:   Rest Day/Catch Up

Faith in Action

Make up your mind to show kindness to those who have not been so kind to you.

Week 17　　　　Date: _____

Journal Questions

1. King Saul is remembered for consulting a medium. What pushed Saul to do this and why are we to stay away from them? What "mediums" do people seek in our day?

2. King David had a powerful prayer in 1 Chronicles 16. Read through the prayer again and write down what aspects of the prayer bring specific encouragement to you today.

3. What was wrong with what David did in 1 Chronicles 21? The weight of David's sin was great to him. How does he respond? What can we learn from this in dealing with our own sin?

4. Ezekiel 18:20 says that we are held accountable for our own sin and not for the sin of others. This seems to be contrary to what happens in the story of 1 Chronicles 21. We know Ezekiel was familiar with these stories and clearly did not see a contradiction. How do you think we might reconcile this?

Week 17
Reflection & Notes

Gratitude

Inspiration

My husband, Ivan, was a logger. His job was on the ground cutting down trees. The days started early for him. Before he left, I would pray with him for protection. We had been praying like that for a whole month. God had told me to do this with my husband in response to my question to Him, "How can I honor my husband." So I had been faithfully praying for his protection every morning before he left for work, declaring, "No weapon formed against him would prosper."

December 15, 2009, was not a typical day. Upon attempting to cut his second tree, my husband's chainsaw got stuck in the tree before he was finished cutting it. He quickly motioned the skidder operator for help. The skidder came and pushed the tree over. The vibration of the tree falling caused a large seventeen foot branch hung up in another nearby tree to come down like an arrow. The branch pierced Ivan in the head, breaking his hard hat into a million little pieces, and putting a golf ball sized hole in the top of his head. The intense pressure inside his head at that moment also caused his brain to break the bone behind his eye, pushing part of his brain into his eye socket. His boss, the skidder operator, saw it happen and ran over to him and declared, "In the name of Jesus, you will not die today!"

They were working down in a deep valley where there was no cell reception, but their 911 call was miraculously able to get out. When the ambulance and fire truck showed up they realized they would not be able to get him to a hospital in time to save his life, so they called for a helicopter. By the grace of God, a medical helicopter from Mayo Clinic was miraculously in the air almost right above them at that moment and dropped down to pick him up. Within seven minutes, they got him to a tiny little hospital that was not usually properly staffed with any doctor that would have been able to save him or give him proper care. Thankfully, that day the top US Army doctor from Bethesda, Pennsylvania, happened to be doing a two week training there and immediately took charge of Ivan's surgery to save his life. He knew exactly what to do, as he had done surgeries of the same kind on countless wounded soldiers. Our pastor overheard him talking to the other doctors, standing his ground and telling them, "No, you are not doing it that way, you are doing it my way."

Ivan's life was miraculously saved that day. God had prepared for a miracle by pre-ordering all the little details in advance to bring about the exact care needed, at the precise time needed. In the moment of our greatest need, God was already there! He was in the hospital a total of sixteen days until he was able to walk again. He suffered paralysis on his right side. Much therapy was needed. In many aspects, he is still in recovery, but today he and I own and operate a cattle ranch running around 1400 animals. God is so good, preparing solutions to problems before they even exist.

~Marilyn Sadlier

"Glory in His holy name; let the hearts of those who seek the Lord rejoice!"
~1 Chronicles 16:10

Week 18

"But as for you, be strong and do not give up, for your work will be rewarded." ~2 Chronicles 15:7

READING PLAN

Day 1:	2 Chronicles 1-3
Day 2:	2 Chronicles 4-7
Day 3:	2 Chronicles 8-10
Day 4:	2 Chronicles 11-13
Day 5:	2 Chronicles 14-16
Day 6:	2 Chronicles 17-19
Day 7:	Rest Day/Catch Up

Faith in Action

Take a moment to confess your sins to the Lord and humble yourself before Him.

Week 18   Date: _____

Journal Questions

1. We are told to pray, humble ourselves, and turn from our wicked ways. Is there any one of these that you have knowingly failed to do? What areas in your life can you humble yourself?

2. As leaders, the kings set the tone for how their people would follow the Lord. What tone are you setting in areas where you have influence?

3. Kings often chose not to rely on God, but instead looked to other things. How often have you made this same mistake? In what ways can you improve in this area?

4. The Queen of Sheba "saw the wisdom of Solomon." (2 Chronicles 9:3) What do you think she saw?

Week 18

Reflection & Notes

Gratitude

Letters To God

My Letter:

His Reply:

Week 19

"You will not need to fight in this battle. Stand firm, hold your position, and see the salvation of the Lord on your behalf, O Judah and Jerusalem." ~2 Chronicles 20:17

READING PLAN

Day 1:	2 Chronicles 20-24
Day 2:	2 Chronicles 25-28
Day 3:	2 Chronicles 29-32
Day 4:	2 Chronicles 33-36
Day 5:	Ezra 1-5
Day 6:	Ezra 6-10
Day 7:	Rest Day/Catch Up

Faith in Action

Take a moment to pray and give the battle to the Lord that you need to surrender to Him. Let Him fight for you.

Week 19   Date: _____

Journal Questions

1. What battles are you fighting right now that belong to the Lord?

2. King Ahab had poor counselors speaking into his life that led him astray from God (2 Chronicles 22:2-5). Who are you allowing to speak into your life, or give you counsel? Does it line up with the Word of God?

3. God calls us to be a "holy" or "set apart" people. Reading through Ezra, is there anything in your life that God may be asking you to shift away from to set yourself apart?

4. Hezekiah was a great king of Israel. He restored Israel back to God's ways. What did it look like to restore things back to God's ways? Are there areas that you need to restore back to God's ways in your own life?

Week 19
Reflection & Notes

Gratitude

INSPIRATION

As a young mother, pain and sickness entered my life through a disease called fibromyalgia. The doctors had no answers. My health steadily declined over the next fourteen years and my little family suffered with me. In a frantic quest for answers, I read over one hundred self-help books. Nevertheless, I continued deteriorating down to 82 pounds as I was only able to eat two food options for three years.

Life flooded out of my body. My core body temperature dropped to 83 degrees. Years of malnutrition, acute sensitivities and numerous allergies wrecked my body and I was crashing. Hospitals terrified me, but in my desperation, I agreed to go.

Triage nurses immediately checked me into critical care, hooked me up to IV therapy and put me on a hot bed. The hospital released me six days later, but complications and reactions to the IV therapy decimated my memory. It was another crushing blow. My husband and I were hopeless.

Two months after my hospital stay, my husband and I happened upon a television preacher we had never watched before. As I listened, my heart burned with hope as they shared, "God desires to do miracles for us because of His immeasurable love." I listened intently as he continued, "If you have lost a family member, if your business has failed, or if you are sick, Jesus wants to answer your prayers." In desperation, I finally cried out to God. I said the sinner's prayer and was born again. I surrendered every one of my weaknesses to God. He came in a powerful light and loved me and forgave me right where I was at.

Jesus directed me to seek prayer for healing. I lay on a sleeping bag in the back of our jeep, as my husband drove to prayer meetings each week. Miracles piled upon miracles as hundreds of believers prayed for me. They instructed me to forgive everyone, including myself, and then God would give me the authority to tell the sickness to leave my body. One year later, my faith grew strong enough to believe God could do anything and to take hold of His promises for healing. I was passionately in love with Jesus! From head to toe, Jesus healed me and saved me when no doctor could figure out my case.

Through the many trials, I learned valuable elements to living a full, rich life: asking this wildly loving Jesus into our hearts and believing He can restore. Jesus is the good news. He wants all of us to know His plan of salvation and to know the riches of His promises. Our hearts can be broken in so many different ways, but our God is in the business of restoration. He can bring you back to life and give you measurably more than what you lost. His big, loving arms can heal the worst of circumstances. If your heart is broken and you are not living the life you hoped for, pray and ask God for salvation. Give your life to Him and He will come into your heart. He is eager to help you. You are meant to run with the King!

~Nancy Ann Johnson, Author of "Ask for Your Miracle"

Week 20

"And who knows whether you have not come to the kingdom for such a time as this?" ~*Esther 4:14*

READING PLAN

Day 1: Nehemiah 1-3
Day 2: Nehemiah 4-7
Day 3: Nehemiah 8-10
Day 4: Nehemiah 11-13
Day 5: Esther 1-3
Day 6: Esther 4-6
Day 7: Rest Day/Catch Up

Faith in Action

Write (or text) someone in your life a "thank you" note telling them you're grateful for them.

Week 20   Date: _____

Journal Questions

1. If there was one thing you could ask God to restore for you personally, what would that be? Why?

2. What's something that stood out to you in the scripture reading this week? What's something you struggled to understand? Pray and ask God to help you have a deeper understanding.

3. In Hebrew, Nehemiah means "God comforts." How is that name relatable to what you read this week? How has He comforted you in your life?

4. God used Esther to protect His people. She had to choose to not stay silent and to go against her society, culture, and the king's policy, yet she found favor. Has there been a time when you needed to speak up or do something hard that may have been contrary to the world, yet He granted you favor? How can you be ready if He asks you to do something like that in the future?

Week 20
Reflection & Notes

Gratitude

Letters To God

My Letter:

His Reply:

Week 21

"Behold, blessed is the one whom God reproves; therefore despise not the discipline of the Almighty." ~Job 5:17

READING PLAN

Day 1:	Esther 7-10
Day 2:	Job 1-3
Day 3:	Job 4-7
Day 4:	Job 8-11
Day 5:	Job 12-14
Day 6:	Job 15-17
Day 7:	Rest Day/Catch Up

Faith in Action

Do you have a testimony to share about how God brought you through a trial, to refine you in Him or to bring you to Him? Write out your testimony so you are prepared to share it as He leads you.

Week 21 Date: _____

Journal Questions

1. Job was stripped away from all his earthly possessions and even suffered physical ailments. If you were in Job's shoes, how would you feel or react? How can we still turn to God and rely on Him in our toughest moments?

2. Has there ever been a time in your life when you wanted to give up? How did you continue forward?

3. What are non-materialistic things you can be thankful for? Write them down and praise Him.

4. Does it seem like either party is listening to the other in the conversation between Job and his friends? Do you tend to intently listen to others when they speak or do you hear just enough to quickly respond and interject your own opinion? How can you become a better listener?

Week 21
Reflection & Notes

Gratitude

Inspiration

Imagine you have been diagnosed with a terminal brain disease. You have been in hospice care longer than the government allows. So, they put you on palliative care, which means they focus on relieving pain without dealing with the cause of the condition. All are waiting for you to die. Then, something happens.

For about a decade, my condition went from bad to worse. I lost the ability to drive, walk, and eat. I almost always needed help. Everyone I loved most, abandoned me. Only my parents and a few friends remained. Life just kept getting worse. I lost my career, car, house, wife and even children. I had nothing and hardly anyone left.

Then, something began to happen when I went for a special heart test. Something seemed different. I asked the nurse what she heard when she listened to my lungs. She just looked at me oddly. I asked again, explaining that no one had been able to hear air movement in my lower quadrants for years. She said she could hear air. "It's a miracle!" I exclaimed! "You're alive! That's a miracle!" she replied. She knew the terminal brain disease I had. Every day I was alive was another miracle.

In fact, I am a literal walking, talking miracle. I soon regained my ability to speak again and even sing. Vocal cords do not heal from atrophy, without a miracle. I began to walk, after being in a wheelchair for a decade. No one just gets up and walks. Yet, I did. I'll admit it wasn't too far at first, but it was farther all the time, until I was mowing the grass alongside the road.

Through this brain disease, I lost the one thing I desired most: marriage and family. I literally lost everything and everyone. I lost the large, nice house I personally designed and built, my farm and all the animals, numerous cars, and a tractor (which is a necessity for a man like me), my career (for which I had trained much of my life), my wife, and my three girls.

Thankfully, God redeems and has restored my life. Now I'm married to someone who loves me unconditionally and I am blessed by her two boys and daughter, a precious girl so much like all the good in all three of mine.

My life is a miracle, every second, of every minute, of every hour, of every day, of every month, of every year! I was not expected to live two years when first diagnosed. When I lived ten years, all were shocked. I have now lived 20 years! I am not yet fully healed. In fact, I am still very sick, but I am healed enough to give others hope. Isn't that a miracle?

If you fail to see miracles, I must ask, "What are you looking for?" or perhaps, "What or who are you looking at?" Miracles are all around us. As the medical staff once said, "You're alive! That's a miracle!" Why do we have to be completely healed for it to be a miracle? Most people are surprised to learn I was ever as sick as I was. After having lived through all I have, let me give you this encouragement, "Live life for YHVH and truly love Him." If you do that, no matter what happens, you will be the miracle!

~*Paul Nandico*

Week 22

"I have not departed from the commandment of His lips; I have treasured the words of His mouth more than my portion of food."
~Job 23:12

READING PLAN

Day 1:	Job 18-21
Day 2:	Job 22-24
Day 3:	Job 25-28
Day 4:	Job 29-31
Day 5:	Job 32-35
Day 6:	Job 36-39
Day 7:	Rest Day/Catch Up

Faith in Action

Is there something that has been a huge distraction for you? Perhaps it has even been distracting you from God. Take time to finish that task this week, remove it, or give yourself a time limit so you can move forward.

Week 22   Date: _____

Journal Questions

1. Job was having back and forth conversations with his friends. They seemed to have different views and opinions. What unshakeable convictions do you have about God that no one can change your mind on?

2. It seems as if God was silent during Job's trials. Job doesn't hear from God again until the end when he repents and God lifts him up. Is there a time when God has felt silent? How have you dealt with that?

3. What can you glean from the story of Job and learn in moments of silence from God?

4. In Job 38, God speaks to Job again. What do you learn about God, His nature and character in these verses?

Week 22
Reflection & Notes

Gratitude

LETTERS TO GOD

My Letter:

His Reply:

Week 23

"And those who know Your Name will put their trust in You, For You, O Lord, have not forsaken those who seek You." ~*Psalm 9:10*

READING PLAN

Day 1:	Job 40-42
Day 2:	Psalms 1-5
Day 3:	Psalms 6-10
Day 4:	Psalms 11-16
Day 5:	Psalms 17-20
Day 6:	Psalms 21-25
Day 7:	Rest Day/Catch Up

Faith in Action

Meditate on His goodness as we wade into Psalms. The Psalms are meant for praise and worship. Find a song that sings one of the Psalms and listen to it throughout the week.

Week 23   Date: _____

Journal Questions

1. We end the book of Job and see his trials and then how God blessed him even greater in the latter days of his life. Is there a time in your life where you went through a hard time and then came out better off? Or if you are currently in a hard time, how can Job's story give you hope?

2. What can you praise God for today? Psalms are our praise and prayers!

3. Righteousness is mentioned often in the scriptures. What is righteousness according to the Bible?

4. God is against evil doings, slander, wickedness, those speaking falsehood, and all forms of sin. Are there areas where you are intentionally walking in sin and struggle to be in communion with God?

Week 23
Reflection & Notes

Gratitude

Inspiration

It was a bright and sunny day in June 2015, when we headed off on a weekend family trip to Elitch Gardens in Denver. While having fun on a water slide ride, I was bounced off the mat I was laying on. Didn't seem like a big deal at that moment, but shortly after I started to feel a sharp pain in my back. In the following days and weeks, it went from being a small, inconsistent pain, to a nagging pain that began to go down my right leg.

Within a few weeks, I wasn't able to sit comfortably or sleep well. It got to the point that when we had friends over, I would rarely sit down because of the pain. I started to go to a chiropractor three times a week, but sadly it did not help at all. I tried a sports therapist, which did help momentarily, but the pain would always return. Out of frustration, I even tried cortisone injections, and still got no relief. The pain continued.

Three years later, I got the opportunity to visit the doctor who had saved my leg when it was crushed in a farm accident when I was 14 years old. I was grateful to see him for my back and hoped he would have some solutions for the pain. He determined I had a herniated disc between L4 and L5. He explained it like this, "Imagine taking a jelly filled donut and squeezing the jelly out. You can never properly get the jelly back in again." He suggested I would need to undergo surgery to restore it. We made plans to do surgery in the spring of 2018.

In the meantime, we went to a prayer and fasting event at our church. While we were there the pastor said, "We will be praying for healing tonight." As soon as he said that, something lit up inside of me and I knew it was for me!

The night took a different turn and we ended up spending a lot of time praying for marriages and closed the night without praying for any healing. I was a little disappointed because I had felt that there was healing for me.

On the second night, as soon as the pastor said, "let's pray for healing." I bolted up and was the first one up at the altar. I didn't want to miss my chance! I felt hands being placed on my shoulders and I heard someone praying over my back. My back started to get extremely hot and I started wondering, "Why did they put a hot pack on my back? That's weird!" Then, at that moment it hit me, "This is happening, this is really happening! This is happening to me!" The pain got so intense I had to go on my knees. I could literally feel my back and spine getting longer. The only way I can explain what happened is "the jelly went back in the donut."

For a few days after it happened, I was doubtful. I kept expecting the pain to come back. I was raised not believing in miracles and I had never experienced anything like that. It was all very new and unexpected. I didn't really tell anyone what had happened for the first few days, even though I was immediately able to sit, bend over and I was able to sleep all night, with absolutely no pain, for the first time in years.

Finally, it really truly hit me that I had been completely healed, and the pain wasn't ever coming back. I have been completely pain free for over four years now. God is still in the business of healing people!

~Ben Miller

Week 24

"Create in me a pure heart, O God, and renew a steadfast spirit within me." ~*Psalm 51:10*

READING PLAN

Day 1:	Psalms 26-30
Day 2:	Psalms 31-35
Day 3:	Psalms 36-40
Day 4:	Psalms 41-45
Day 5:	Psalms 46-50
Day 6:	Psalms 51-55
Day 7:	Rest Day/Catch Up

Faith in Action

Pray and ask God to show you the goodness in His Word as you read the Psalms. We are called to meditate on His Word day and night.

Week 24   Date: _____

Journal Questions

1. David talks about fearing God often in the Psalms. What does it mean to "fear God?"

2. King David walked through many trials in his lifetime, but through it all he chose to praise God. What are ways you can praise God even in the hard times?

3. In chapter 19 the Psalmist concludes by saying, "May the words of my mouth and the meditation of my heart be pleasing to You..." Reflect on the meditation of your heart. Is it pleasing to Him?

4. Psalm 20:4 states, "May He grant you your heart's desire and fulfill all your plans." What are your plans and desires? Do they line up with God's heart and character as we see in the Scriptures?

Week 24
Reflection & Notes

Gratitude

Letters To God

My Letter:

His Reply:

Week 25

"He only is my rock and my salvation, my fortress; I shall not be shaken." ~*Psalm 62:6*

READING PLAN

Day 1:	Psalms 56-60
Day 2:	Psalms 61-65
Day 3:	Psalms 66-70
Day 4:	Psalms 71-75
Day 5:	Psalms 76-78
Day 6:	Psalms 79-85
Day 7:	Rest Day/Catch Up

Faith in Action

Take action to bring a person solace this week by sending a note of encouragement, volunteering to babysit, or paying for lunch, etc.

Week 25 Date: _____

Journal Questions

1. Psalm 50 speaks to "my people" and "the wicked." Compare and contrast what God says to His people versus those who walk in wickedness?

2. God does not promise us an easy life but rather to always be with us, to sustain us, to comfort us, and that the end with Him is better than any riches of the earth. How can you lean in more and trust Him with your life?

3. What are three lessons from Psalm 78 that you can learn for yourself and pass on to future generations?

4. Psalm 66:10 says that "God has proved us and refined us as silver." What does it mean to be refined? Do you have an example from your life?

Week 25
Reflection & Notes

Gratitude

INSPIRATION

Let me tell you about the time God said, "LIVE," and I did!

In the Fall of 2010, I was driving home and was only two streets away from pulling in the driveway. I had kicked off my shoes, calling it a night, and then suddenly found myself on the way to Shock Trauma where doctors were fighting to save my life. It had been a horrific car accident. So horrific, my car flipped several times before landing right side up. I can remember climbing out of the passenger side window before collapsing on the side of the road in severe pain. I was in too much pain to move.

By the grace of God, one of our neighbors went for a drive around the neighborhood at 10pm. He found me on the side of the road, unconscious. Minutes later, I was at the local ER. They didn't feel equipped to save me so they sent me to Shock Trauma because I had so much internal bleeding. I didn't realize until then all ER's are not the same. There are ER's and there are Trauma Centers for more life-threatening cases requiring a team of physicians. The latter was my case.

I recall asking the doctors at Shock Trauma, "Am I going to make it?" They responded, "We don't know." I had many injuries; hematoma, pneumothorax, six broken ribs, a spliced spleen, and a severely damaged liver. The liver was my main problem. The doctors told my husband, "It was as if someone took her liver and lifted it up and then threw it on the ground. There are so many splices in it." They would need to do an extensive laser surgery to put my liver back together. Doctors also said I would need to be completely still the entire time. As they wheeled me into the surgery room, the song, "What a Beautiful Word" played in the background. To this day, this song takes me back, reminding me of the hope I gripped onto that day and never let go of.

After the liver surgery, an infection took hold of my liver. Doctors told my husband I was not going to make it unless they put a drain in my liver. They said it was a risky procedure with no guarantee it would work. I would have to remain there for several more months. At this point, I had already been there two and a half weeks, remembering very little of that time as I was on so many pain meds. My family was devastated, scared, and desperate for me to be okay.

The day prior to my liver drain surgery, my husband called his workplace to share updates with his colleague. She said to him, "Pray Ezekiel 16:6 over her!" The passage reads, "And when I passed by you and saw you struggling in your own blood, I said to you in your blood, 'Live!'" She told him it worked for her nephew. My husband, already at the hospital with a roomful of visitors, including our pastor and children, formed a circle around me. Our pastor read Ezekiel 16:6 over me and everyone prayed. I vaguely remember thinking during their prayer circle, "I wish I could take their fear and pain away."

As I was being prepped for surgery the next morning, the trauma doctors arrived saying, "It's inexplicable! Nothing short of a miracle! The infection is gone! She will make it." It has been almost twelve years since my accident. God said, "Live" and I've been living ever since. And I will continue to live the abundant life until He calls me home!

~Michelle Rene' Hammer, MS, LCPC

Week 26

"He who dwells in the shelter of the Most High will abide in the shadow of the Almighty. I will say to the Lord, 'My refuge and my fortress, my God, in whom I trust.'" ~*Psalm 91:1-2*

READING PLAN

Day 1:	Psalms 86-89
Day 2:	Psalms 90-95
Day 3:	Psalms 96-100
Day 4:	Psalms 101-105
Day 5:	Psalms 106-108
Day 6:	Psalms 109-113
Day 7:	Rest Day/Catch Up

Faith in Action

Pick one of the Psalms you read this week, write it out by hand and put it up where you can see it daily.

Week 26   Date: _____

Journal Questions

1. Many of the Psalms mention "idols" or "other gods." Idols often can be a figure or statue that people worship, however it can also be anything that we raise up above God, such as money, work, exercise, ourselves, family, or friendships. What idols do you struggle with in your life??

2. What are some promises that you enjoyed reading about in the Psalms this week?

3. Psalm 91:4 says, "God is our shield and protector." How has He protected you in your life?

4. If we love God, we are to hate evil. How do we hate evil, and yet love our neighbor if they act in evil ways?

Week 26
Reflection & Notes

Gratitude

Letters To God

My Letter:

His Reply:

Week 27

"I lift up my eyes to the hills. From where does my help come? My help comes from the Lord, who made heaven and earth."
~Psalm 121:1-2

READING PLAN

Day 1:	Psalms 114-118
Day 2:	Psalms 119
Day 3:	Psalms 120-127
Day 4:	Psalms 128-133
Day 5:	Psalms 134-139
Day 6:	Psalms 140-144
Day 7:	Rest Day/Catch Up

Faith in Action

Congratulations! You are halfway through reading the Bible! Spend an extra 20 minutes this week journaling about what God is teaching you through your scripture readings.

Week 27 Date: _____

Journal Questions

1. A great way to praise God in times of trouble is to recount all the blessings and things He has already done for us. What prayers has the Lord already answered? What are some things He has already done for you, specifically?

2. Several Psalms reveal a prophetic promise of the coming Messiah. What do we learn about Jesus, our Messiah, in Psalm 110?

3. In reading through the Psalms, what does love look like to God? How does King David show God love, and how does God show love to him, and us?

4. What does it look like to trust God, to truly trust Him? What would look different in your life if you trusted Him fully? How can your actions and words reflect that you trust Him?

Week 27
Reflection & Notes

Gratitude

Inspiration

It was a miracle crusade night in Uganda, Africa. Thousands gathered to hear the Word of God and to receive their miracles. Others came because they had heard of the miracles that happened the night before. And others were on-lookers, not knowing what to expect. Most certainly there were witches and warlocks present as they usually are on any given crusade night.

This night felt different. There was a sense of expectation in the air. An expectIon of a great move of God. As I preached the word that night, I felt the Lord say to me to release His glory over the people. As I did, the Lord began to download words of knowledge: tumors disappearing, infertility curses nullified, blind eyes open, deaf and dumb set free, foul spirits and demonic oppression broken, in the mighty name of Jesus. Those who were mentally tormented by evil spirits began to manifest.

After releasing the glory of God, I felt led to have those who had received their miracle come to the platform to testify. Suddenly, a mama began to bring her child up the steps of the platform as I was speaking to the crowd. I felt her presence behind me. I immediately turned around and saw her holding her child. I then felt a special anointing surge in me and I heard the Holy Spirit say, "She will walk!" I knew in my spirit I was about to see the Lord perform a miracle.

I looked at the mama and her child and reached out my hand to her and said, "Bring her to me!" The mama immediately brought her to me. While the mom continued to hold her, I directed two of my team members to each put one of their hands on each of the little girl's feet. I declared, "In the mighty name of Jesus, I command the spirit of infirmity and paralysis to come out of her now! Little girl, I command you to walk!" I stretched out my hand and said, "Mama give her to me!" The mom gave me the girl's hands and I immediately assisted her across the platform as she took her very first steps.

Her name was Devine. Devine was a four-year-old girl who had never walked from birth. Devine was miraculously healed that night and walked for the very first time. My eyes were filled with tears and my voice cracked as I testified to the crowd of what had just taken place. Thousands of people witnessed this miracle. Devine's life was transformed from that day forward and she will never be the same. As a result of Devine's miracle, thousands gave their lives to the Lord that night and their lives were transformed forever.

Moving in miracles does not take a superwoman or a superman. It simply takes a person willing to listen to the voice of God and obey without question. It takes obedience and faith to see miracles happen. The Lord's will is always to heal. Sometimes we don't see miracles because we don't believe. Sometimes we don't see miracles because it's not the right time and God is in the process of doing something. Whatever the reason, we should never give up pursuing miracles.

Inevitably your miracle will come. In God's timing it will come. In fact, it's already on the way. He will not leave you and will always back up His Word. When you make a declaration, heaven is mobilized and invades earth. We get to see the kingdom of God come to earth when miracles happen. In heaven there is no sin or infirmity. Let us, together, contend to see a mighty move of God upon the earth today. Let us partner with heaven and co-create with God. Let heaven on earth become our reality.

~Apostle Jessica Z. Maldonado, Founder: Freedom To The Nations - FreedomToTheNations.org

Week 28

"The fear of the Lord is the beginning of knowledge, but fools despise wisdom and instruction." ~*Proverbs 1:7*

READING PLAN

Day 1:	Psalms 145-150
Day 2:	Proverbs 1-3
Day 3:	Proverbs 4-7
Day 4:	Proverbs 8-11
Day 5:	Proverbs 12-14
Day 6:	Proverbs 15-17
Day 7:	Rest Day/Catch Up

Faith in Action

Make a list of those who may need your forgiveness and ask God to walk you through forgiving them.

Week 28 Date: _____

Journal Questions

1. What is wisdom according to Scripture? What are some differences between wisdom from God and wisdom from the world?

2. As believers, how do we stray from evil and stay in the ways of the Lord? What are some things God hates, and seem unwise, that we are warned to stay away from in Proverbs?

3. What is pride in God's eyes? What is humility?

4. While reading this week, what thoughts came up that you need to change or get rid of so that they don't become a stumbling block, or lead to foolishness? Ask for forgiveness, pray, and seek Him on how to grow in wisdom.

Week 28
Reflection & Notes

Gratitude

Letters To God

My Letter:

His Reply:

Week 29

"Death and life are in the power of the tongue, and those who love it will eat its fruits." ~*Proverbs 18:21*

READING PLAN

Day 1:	Proverbs 18-21
Day 2:	Proverbs 22-24
Day 3:	Proverbs 25-27
Day 4:	Proverbs 28-31
Day 5:	Ecclesiastes 1-4
Day 6:	Ecclesiastes 5-8
Day 7:	Rest Day/Catch Up

Faith in Action

Pray and ask God to help you become a God-fearing believer.

Week 29 Date: _____

Journal Questions

1. God cares about what comes out of your mouth and how you control your tongue. Slander and gossip are sin in God's eyes. Are you guilty of this? What are steps you can take to change these habits?

2. You finished Proverbs this week. What Proverb stood out to you the most and you feel God used to speak to you? Why do you feel it spoke to you?

3. If you are man who is married, write out Proverbs 31:10-31 and pray this over your wife as a blessing. If you are a woman who is married, write this out and pray for God to refine you into a Proverbs 31 wife.

4. According to Ecclesiastes 3, everything has a time and season appointed by God. Recognizing the season you are in can give you clarity, focus, and the ability to prepare for the next season. What season are you in right now? What are ways you can be better prepared for it?

Week 29
Reflection & Notes

Gratitude

INSPIRATION

I was twenty-six years old the first time I woke up with hands so red and swollen I could barely move them. Tying my toddlers' little shoes with wiggling feet was difficult. I had three small children under the age of seven to take care of. I didn't have time to think about my hands that morning. I got up and going as best I could. Sippy cups don't fill themselves and diapers have to be changed, no matter how clumsy you feel, with swollen, aching hands.

I thought that morning was a fluke. I wondered if I had slept on my hands in a strange position or eaten too much salt the day before, but the symptoms continued for months. The pain intensified every morning and began to spread to the rest of my body. Before long I was waking up with swollen hands, feet, ankles, and knees. Three months after the pain began, I could no longer squeeze the shampoo out of the container by myself, open a water bottle, tie my children's shoes or turn the key in my car's ignition.

When you're in your mid-twenties, it's hard to accept that anything might be seriously wrong, even when that's exactly what your body is clearly telling you. I knew I couldn't avoid it any longer and scheduled a visit with a specialist. My fears were confirmed when the doctor informed me that I had an incurable autoimmune disease called rheumatoid arthritis. It's difficult to explain the wave of emotions that come over you when you learn your body is attacking itself.

I spent six agonizing years trying to adapt to a perpetual state of physical, mental and emotional exhaustion. I struggled every day just to accomplish basic tasks. I dreamed of sleeping seven hours and waking up with enough energy and strength to put on makeup or fix my hair and feel like a "normal" woman. I wanted so desperately to take my babies to the park and push them on the swings without being totally wiped out. Simple activities like bike rides, jumping on the trampoline, or taking a day to go fishing required too much energy. Trying to do everyday family activities typically meant I'd spend the next three days in bed with a flare-up or end up with some kind of illness or infection.

After six years, I decided I'd had enough. I was angry about all the years I'd "missed" and I was determined not to miss any more. I knew God wanted more for me. My healing journey with God took time. It was fraught with trial and error as well as prayer and obedience. I had to learn to open my heart and mind to listen for the instructions Jehovah Rapha, the God who heals, gave me. Today I am completely healed. I have not had any symptoms nor medication for almost eleven years. My doctors said curing my disease was impossible. My God says all things are possible.

God is still a God of miracles. Sometimes healing happens instantly. Other times, as in my case, God invites us to partner with Him in our healing as He gives us specific instructions for our journey. Both forms of healing are miraculous. Accept the invitation from Jesus to embark on your own journey to healing and I believe there will be a radical breakthrough in your body, mind, and spirit. Jesus clearly tells us what He desires for us all in John 10:10: "I came that they may have life and have it abundantly."

~Dafne Wiswell

Week 30

"Fear God and keep His commandments, for this is the duty of all mankind." ~*Ecclesiastes 12:13*

READING PLAN

Day 1:	Ecclesiastes 9-12
Day 2:	Song of Solomon 1-4
Day 3:	Song of Solomon 5-8
Day 4:	Isaiah 1-4
Day 5:	Isaiah 5-8
Day 6:	Isaiah 9-12
Day 7:	Rest Day/Catch Up

Faith in Action

Write a letter to God and thank Him for the opportunity to be reading His Word. Many people have lived their whole lives without having that opportunity.

Week 30 Date: _____

Journal Questions

1. In Ecclesiastes 11:4 laziness and lack of effort does not give us the fruit or results we desire. Are you not seeing results or fruit because you're not doing the things that need to be done? How can you shift into being active to start reaping the fruit you want in your life?

2. Our relationship with God is seen as a marriage covenant. What do you think are a few keys to a good, loving marriage? What did you learn about our relationship with God through the illustration of marriage in the Song of Solomon?

3. Jesus and our Salvation was the plan from the beginning. What prophecies of Jesus do we see in the first few chapters of Isaiah? (Look at chapters 4, 7, 9, 11.)

4. How does Isaiah 5:20 apply to today? How can we keep ourselves protected from this deception?

Week 30
Reflection & Notes

Gratitude

Letters To God

My Letter:

His Reply:

Week 31

"O Lord, You are my God. I will exalt You; I will praise Your name, for You have done wonderful things, plans formed of old, faithful and sure." ~*Isaiah 25:1*

READING PLAN

Day 1:	Isaiah 13-16
Day 2:	Isaiah 17-20
Day 3:	Isaiah 21-24
Day 4:	Isaiah 25-27
Day 5:	Isaiah 28-31
Day 6:	Isaiah 32-35
Day 7:	Rest Day/Catch Up

Faith in Action

Encourage three people this week through an act of service, gift, a sweet note, or message.

Week 31　　　　Date: _____

Journal Questions

1. Part of the prophecy of Isaiah was a warning to people of certain lands to heed the voice of the Lord. Has there been a time when God has warned you to heed His voice? Did you hear and obey? What became of the situation?

2. Even in judgment and hardship, God always leaves a remnant. What does He seek and speak about the remnant in Isaiah 10:20?

3. What are some things we learn about God and His character in these chapters of Isaiah? What are things He is not pleased with?

4. Isaiah 29 prophecies of those that "draw near with their lips but their heart is far from Me." How do the two compare: drawing near with your lips versus drawing near with your heart?

Week 31
Reflection & Notes

Gratitude

Inspiration

My whole life changed when the doctor said, "I'm sorry, but there is nothing that can be done about your nerve damage. You will not regain the abilities in your legs." Fear consumed me while sitting there in my wheelchair, until I heard a voice say, "But, you serve a God who heals!" The second I agreed with that statement, the fear completely left.

One day, a friend came over to lay hands on me, and as she prayed she said, "I keep seeing you dancing in a flower field." Her vision gave me hope.

Months passed by. I stumbled online upon a picture of a woman dancing in a flower field. It was a women's retreat that was happening in the three days. When I called the number they said, "We actually had a cancellation today and have one spot!"

At the retreat, the pastor came over to me in my walker and asked, "How did you hear about us?" I heard a powerful voice yell in my mind, "Do not tell them that you are here to be healed because when you are not, everyone's faith will be on the line!" I fought against the fear and yelled out, "I am here to be healed and I am supposed to dance in that flower field!" The whole room went crazy yelling, "Amen! Yes Lord! Heal her Lord!"

A bit later, a young lady prayed for me and said, "Oh honey, the Lord wants you to deal with this unforgiveness." Another woman prayed and cried because she said she saw a seven-year-old boy with dark hair who had a spirit of murder and suicide on him. I immediately knew she was talking about my son. He talked about those things all the time. I asked where the spirit came from? She replied, "His name sake?" I asked her how to get rid of it. She said, "You just ask Jesus. It's His will to set your son free." I asked the Lord to heal my baby and immediately I could feel the heaviness come off of me. I knew healing happened at that moment for my son. The other woman asked, "Who do you need to forgive?" I replied, "I need to forgive my father, who committed suicide when I was pregnant with my son, whom I named him after." As soon as I forgave my father, peace overwhelmed me.

At midnight, the pastor announced it was time to leave the room. I immediately told the Lord, "Your Word says You will not put your servant to shame. Please do not allow me to leave without dancing in that flower field." Just then, a little girl walked up to me and asked if she could pray for me. I knew this would be the final breakthrough. She said, "Jesus will you heal her so she can go back and show the doctors that Jesus still heals in Jesus name, amen!" Something happened at that moment! I asked Jesus, "I've been asking You all day to let me run to You. Will you just let me run to You?" I immediately felt an alignment in my hips and my back. I moved the walker to the side. I lifted one leg and it was light. I lifted the next leg and it was light! I began to run and kept running while screaming, "THANK YOU, JESUS!"

The Lord healed me that day! When I got home to share what Lord had done with my family, my seven-year-old son came over and sat next to me. He did not even look the same. There was this new found peace in his eyes. He said to me, "Jesus wants me to tell you that my heart is happy now." That child had been transformed, which was another beautiful miracle! And God wasn't finished with His miracles for our family. I gave birth to a baby girl on the one year anniversary date of my healing because the Lord wanted me to always remember and celebrate what He did that day!

~Jennifer Loza

Week 32

"But those who wait on the Lord will renew their strength. They will soar on wings like eagles; they run and are not weary, they walk and do not faint." ~Isaiah 40:31

READING PLAN

Day 1:	Isaiah 36-39
Day 2:	Isaiah 40-42
Day 3:	Isaiah 43-46
Day 4:	Isaiah 47-49
Day 5:	Isaiah 50-53
Day 6:	Isaiah 54-57
Day 7:	Rest Day/Catch Up

Faith in Action

Share the story of salvation with someone or write out what He has done for you so you are ready to share with someone in the future.

Week 32 Date: _____

Journal Questions

1. Isaiah 40 says that grass fades away and dies, flowers bloom and die, but the Word of God stands forever. How can this verse encourage you in whatever you are currently going through?

2. Isaiah 40:11 "He feeds His flock like a shepherd..." What is a shepherd, what is their role, and how do they care for their flock? How does a flock respond to their shepherd? What does it reveal to you about God?

3. God is over all, in all, and sees all. His ways are higher and greater than anything we can come up with on our own. Are you relying on His ways? How can you rely on His ways more than you have been?

4. Isaiah 53 is a prophecy about the Messiah and our salvation. What has the Messiah done for you in your life?

Week 32
Reflection & Notes

Gratitude

Letters To God

My Letter:

His Reply:

Week 33

"The Spirit of the Lord God is upon me, because the Lord has anointed me to bring good news to the poor; he has sent me to bind up the brokenhearted, to proclaim liberty to the captives, and the opening of the prison to those who are bound." ~*Isaiah 61:1*

READING PLAN

Day 1:	Isaiah 58-60
Day 2:	Isaiah 61-63
Day 3:	Isaiah 64-66
Day 4:	Jeremiah 1-3
Day 5:	Jeremiah 4-6
Day 6:	Jeremiah 7-11
Day 7:	Rest Day/Catch Up

Faith in Action

Pray for people in your life that do not know or follow God. Pray for their eyes to be opened to His goodness and love.

Week 33   Date: _____

Journal Questions

1. We have a choice in our walk with God, to follow His ways or our own. In what ways are you following Him? In what ways do you need to stop walking in your own ways and choose His instead?

2. We are told to tremble at His Word. What does this mean and how can you apply it to your life? (Isaiah 66:5, Jeremiah 5:22)

3. Jeremiah was sent to deliver an unpopular message to the people, but God promised to be with him. In what ways have you lost things or felt pressured because of following God? He promises to be with you.

4. Jeremiah 7 speaks of "trusting in false words from people speaking falsely." This still happens today. Falsehood doesn't profit. How can we recognize it? How can you protect against it?

Week 33

Reflection & Notes

Gratitude

Inspiration

After surrendering my life to Christ at eighteen years old, I developed multiple female health problems. At first, I thought these were consequences from my life before Jesus. These problems left me wondering if I'd ever be able to live out my dream of becoming a mom. Throughout the following decade these problems escalated into chronic pain. This pain felt like fire was burning on the inside of me. Days were uncomfortable and nights were tormenting. My only option was to cling to Jesus and His promises. He became my everything and He helped me see these trials were my path to restoration and redemption.

Doctors could not figure out the root of the chronic pain and eventually diagnosed me with nerve pain. The only option for pain management was heavy nerve blockers also known as antidepressants. This medication lowered my pain to a level two, but left me fatigued all day long, even after sleeping ten hours a night. When most young adults are thriving in their twenties, I was undergoing my wilderness season learning to rely on Jesus for everything. Inner healing was my favorite pain remedy during this time, bringing me into a deep intimacy with Jesus as He healed the many wounds of my heart.

God also gave me the faith to believe I would have children, and a husband. He gave me their names to pray for them by faith, yes, even my future husband's name. Nine months after praying for my husband by name, he walked into the church I had been working at. All he had to do was introduce himself as "Anthony" and I knew he was the one I had been praying for. We got married a year later.

I quickly discovered my husband's faith was greater than mine. A few months into our marriage, he was determined to set me free from my infirmity and see me get off the terrible medication I was on. He led me in prayer and commanded an unclean spirit off of me. Immediately, I saw in the spirit a thorny bush unravel itself off my waist and slink away like a snake. I was shocked! Mainly because I didn't think I could have an evil spirit oppressing me since I was full of the Holy Spirit. I learned a good lesson that day.

He encouraged me to take a leap of faith and not take my meds that night. I followed his advice and by the next morning I was overcome by level nine pain. As I reached for my meds that night I heard the Holy Spirit prompt me to ask my husband first. I went to my husband and told him, "I'm taking my meds tonight!" He suggested we pray again. How could I say no? He led me in an encounter with the Father where He said the words, "Whether you take the medication or not, I will be with you." His words comforted me and strengthened my faith.

I decided to not take the meds one more night. The next day, no pain! And the next day, no pain! The third day of no pain, I knew I was healed! Three months later, we got pregnant with our first miracle baby. God did it with no help from doctors. Today, we have two beautiful, healthy children and are expecting our third. "O LORD, you have brought up my soul from Sheol; you restored me to life from among those who go down to the pit." Psalm 30:2. Glory be to the One who has the miracle working power!

~Brit Coppa

Week 34

"For I know the plans I have for you, declares the Lord, plans for welfare and not for evil, to give you a future and a hope."
~Jeremiah 29:11

READING PLAN

Day 1:	Jeremiah 12-15
Day 2:	Jeremiah 16-19
Day 3:	Jeremiah 20-22
Day 4:	Jeremiah 23-26
Day 5:	Jeremiah 27-30
Day 6:	Jeremiah 31-34
Day 7:	Rest Day/Catch Up

Faith in Action

How can you help the poor, orphan and widow more than you are now? Make a plan on how you can help and act on it.

Week 34 Date: _____

Journal Questions

1. Jeremiah was warning the people of what was to come, but God told them if they turned back He would remember their sin no more. Throughout the Bible God makes these types of if-then statements. Have you ever had God speak to you in this type of way? Describe.

2. God calls us to care for the poor, widow, and orphan and to not be greedy with gain. No matter your situation, how can you support the poor, widow and orphan?

3. Jeremiah 31 is the prophecy of the new covenant. This is the covenant we are in now that our Savior has come and died for us. Read and meditate on this chapter. Describe the new covenant.

4. It seems there's a pattern of God's people seeing Him work miracles, saving them, and then they forget and fall away. Why is it so easy for us to forget what He has done for us? Do you easily forget? How can you remember?

Week 34
Reflection & Notes

Gratitude

Letters To God

My Letter:

His Reply:

Week 35

"It is He who made the earth by His power, who established the world by His wisdom, and by His understanding stretched out the heavens." ~*Jeremiah 51:15*

READING PLAN

Day 1:	Jeremiah 35-37
Day 2:	Jeremiah 38-41
Day 3:	Jeremiah 42-45
Day 4:	Jeremiah 46-49
Day 5:	Jeremiah 50-52
Day 6:	Lamentations 1-2
Day 7:	Rest Day/Catch Up

Faith in Action

Pray and ask God to show you where you are trying to return to bondage or what bondage needs to be broken off.

Week 35   Date: _____

Journal Questions

1. Jeremiah was beaten, put in prison, and eventually killed for speaking the words of God and begging people to repent. He was in a dark place. He could have given up on God, but he didn't. How have you handled the dark times in your life? Did you turn away from God?

2. A few people wanted Jeremiah to seek God for them and tell them what to do. Jeremiah came back with a message and warned them not to go back to Egypt. Egypt represented bondage. He warned them not to go back to bondage. What bondage has God delivered you from and what can you do to make sure you never turn back to it?

3. In Jeremiah 51:45, God tells Israel to come out of Babylon. Babylon represents the world and its lusts. How have you come out of Babylon? Are there ways or areas you still need to "come out of Babylon?"

4. It is easy for us to trust in our own works and treasures. It feels comfortable. How can you better trust in His works and treasures versus your own? What are His works and treasures in your life?

Week 35
Reflection & Notes

Gratitude

INSPIRATION

God moves in miraculous ways. That was the conviction in our hearts when we moved from Vancouver in British-Columbia to pastor a small but vibrant congregation in Sherbrooke, Quebec. Six months into our new ministry appointment, the global pandemic struck. All public gatherings, including church services, were prohibited for several months. In the Fall of 2021, our government allowed churches to hold small worship gatherings with no more than 25 people. On a cold Sunday morning, a man with a cane walked into our intimate worship service and quietly sat among us. According to sanitary regulations we were at maximum capacity. Regardless, the greeter at the door had welcomed this stranger and allowed him to attend. That welcome would change his life forever.

Steve was a broken man who had experienced severe trauma. In his early twenties, he decided to become a priest. He joined a Catholic order and lived in a monastery. Because he was articulate and enthusiastic about the message of salvation, one of the nuns dubbed him "Stephen of the Gospel Proclamation." Unfortunately, once he completed his probationary stay at the monastery, he was told by his spiritual directors that monastic life wasn't for him.

He was disappointed and angry. Rather than seeking how to channel his faith in new ways, Steve rebelled against God. However, his recovery and his life remained unstable, marked by addiction relapses, money problems, sexual immorality, and spiritual emptiness.

He eventually made his way to northern Quebec where he hoped to have a fresh start. It is there he was lured by a colleague to a party that turned into a terrifying scene. He was savagely assaulted by a group of men and left for dead, naked in a snowbank. Steve should have died that night, but during the ordeal he cried out to God to deliver him. Steve eventually recovered from the assault, but was left with deep psychological and physical injuries.

A few months later, he walked into our church, now homeless, struggling with severe PTSD, a permanent hip injury and a limp, and chronic pain which he managed with a daily cocktail of medication. At the end of the church service, we asked him if he would like to receive prayer for his leg, assuring him we had witnessed other miraculous healings before. He accepted. We gathered a few believers around and laid hands on him. Our guest immediately felt the power of God at work. The chronic pain in his body left him and instantly he could walk perfectly straight. He was flabbergasted and so were the believers around him who had never or rarely witnessed an instantaneous healing. Afterwards, we bought him lunch, dropped him off at the local shelter, and arranged to meet again with him that week. Over the following weeks we learned his story, he gave his life to Jesus, we did inner healing prayer with him, and even took him out shopping for new clothes. That divine appointment, on a chilly Sunday morning, became a discipleship relationship.

Steve has since moved away, but we have remained in contact. With God's grace he weaned off the pain meds, has given up sexual immorality, and fought his way back from a drug relapse. He called us recently to plan a date for his water baptism. He insisted on doing it at the church that welcomed and accepted him, and dared to love him with prayers of faith, a meal, and lasting friendship. This was a miracle the pandemic couldn't stop.

~Caroline Duocher

Week 36

"And I will give them one heart, and a new spirit I will put within them. I will remove the heart of stone from their flesh and give them a heart of flesh." ~Ezekiel 11:19

READING PLAN

Day 1:	Lamentations 3-5
Day 2:	Ezekiel 1-3
Day 3:	Ezekiel 4-7
Day 4:	Ezekiel 8-11
Day 5:	Ezekiel 12-15
Day 6:	Ezekiel 16-18
Day 7:	Rest Day/Catch Up

Faith in Action

Pray daily for discernment, "God, please give me eyes to see Your truth and ears to hear Your words. God, please allow me to have a discerning spirit and recognize Your truth above all else. Amen."

Week 36   Date: _____

Journal Questions

1. The beginning of Ezekiel shares a vision he had of God and how He is holy. What does "holy" mean in Hebrew? Do you treat and perceive your relationship with God in the holiness He deserves?

2. Ezekiel was given a message by God and was told to deliver it even though they wouldn't listen. Who are you assigned to in your life to give a message from God? (Children, co-workers, family, friends, clients?) Are you sharing it even if they aren't always receptive?

3. In Ezekiel 16, God reminds the people of all that He had done for them. He made them His lovely bride, but the Israelites went astray following their own lusts and trusting in themselves. When things are going well and right, do you tend to stay near to God and give Him the glory, or do you turn to yourself and put God "back up on the shelf?"

4. God warns about false prophets all throughout Scripture. According to Ezekial, who does God consider a false prophet? (Ezekiel 13)

Week 36
Reflection & Notes

Gratitude

Letters To God

My Letter:

His Reply:

Week 37

"I will sprinkle clean water on you, and you shall be clean from all your uncleannesses, and from all your idols I will cleanse you."
~Ezekiel 36:25

READING PLAN

Day 1:	Ezekiel 19-21
Day 2:	Ezekiel 22-24
Day 3:	Ezekiel 25-28
Day 4:	Ezekiel 29-32
Day 5:	Ezekiel 33-36
Day 6:	Ezekiel 37-39
Day 7:	Rest Day/Catch Up

Faith in Action

Study about the Sabbath and pray and ask God what it means for you in your walk with Him.

Week 37 Date: _____

Journal Questions

1. God talks about the Sabbath often as "My Sabbath(s)" and as a "sign between Me and you" (Ezekiel 20:20). Why do you think He would call it His? (Verses to reference: Genesis 1:3, Exodus 16:26, 20:8, 31:15-16, Leviticus 19:3,13, 26:2, Deuteronomy 5:12, Isaiah 58:13, 66:23, Ezekiel 22:8, Matthew 12:8-12, 24:20, Mark 2:27, Acts 15:21, Hebrews 4:9.)

2. Do you keep a Sabbath? Why or why not? What would it look and feel like if you did?

3. Ezekiel prophesied to the leaders that they were leading the people astray. We are all leaders in some way. How can we heed this warning as leaders? In what ways can we unknowingly lead someone astray?

4. What are qualities of a good leader? How can you develop those qualities in your own life?

Week 37
Reflection & Notes

Gratitude

Inspiration

In December 2021, I went to the urgent care with severe cramps and bleeding. I was in menopause, so I had not menstruated for two years at that point. The attending health care workers had no idea why I was bleeding, but I soaked up so much blood in one week they were worried I had a tumor. I had not seen a gynecologist in years and they urged me to make an appointment with one immediately. At my visit, they did several tests and ruled out many possible diagnoses. An ultrasound showed nothing out of the ordinary at first, but when the gynecologist looked further into my results, he found the cause of my problems was my uterine lining which was surprisingly now on the exterior of my uterus and would need to be removed.

My husband started a new job with medical benefits the year before and I was happy to finally have health insurance to help cover the costs. However, when the scheduling nurse told me what my share of expenses were I was dumbfounded. The procedure would cost $3,000 providing there were no complications during surgery and a $5,000 deductible was due prior to surgery. I reluctantly scheduled the surgery and prayed for God's protection and provision.

We sold furniture to raise money for my upcoming surgery, but failed to raise enough funds by the March 3rd deadline we had. My husband feared that I might die without the surgery, but I reassured him that, with prayer, I could be healed. I watched people receive healing from various ailments and diseases and I started to believe I too could be healed with prayer. On March 28, 2021, Sean Feaucht from "Let Us Worship" came to Greensboro, NC to have a revival. I was so happy to go, remembering fondly attending revivals with my grandparents as a child. I eagerly anticipated the thrill and excitement as the preaching started and could already hear the beautiful worship music. I envisioned the deliverances that would take place, the crying out to God to be saved, the miraculous healings. The Lord was there with all of who came to worship Him on that beautiful Palm Sunday and many people were healed. Glory be to God for those healings!

I stood beside a lady from my church named Elizabeth and worshiped with her. Worshippers were instructed to lay their hands on the sick as they prayed. I raised my hand to receive prayer and many hands came to rest upon me, including those of my twelve year old daughter, whom I had brought with me. As they prayed, I felt a tingling and burning sensation surge from the top of my head to my toes. It was a "wow" moment for sure with the Lord. I looked down and saw my friend Elizabeth's hand palm side down over my stomach and her hand was shaking profusely. I knew that day I was healed! I exclaimed over and over again, "Thank you Father for my healing!" The Holy Spirit told me to believe God can heal when we pray.

One month later, I shared the details of my healing with my Thursday night prayer group. My friend Elizabeth said, "You know dear, that was all God!" She explained how a force placed her hand over my stomach and would not let her remove it. Praise the Lord! His Word is mighty! We just have to believe it is His will to heal when we pray. I called my doctor's office the following week and told his nurse I was healed by God and would not need surgery after all!

~Terri Adwell

Week 38

"How great are His signs, how mighty His wonders! His kingdom is an everlasting kingdom, and His dominion endures from generation to generation." ~Daniel 4:3

READING PLAN

Day 1:	Ezekiel 40-42
Day 2:	Ezekiel 43-45
Day 3:	Ezekiel 46-48
Day 4:	Daniel 1-4
Day 5:	Daniel 5-8
Day 6:	Daniel 9-12
Day 7:	Rest Day/Catch Up

Faith in Action

Step outside of yourself this week and do an act of service to help someone in need.

Week 38 Date: _____

Journal Questions

1. Nothing unclean is to be in or around His temple (Ezekiel 44). His Spirit lives in us. What unclean thing is "in your temple" that He may be asking you to let go of? Is there anything you are secretly hiding? He's waiting for you to release it so you can be clean and pure before Him.

2. In Daniel 3, the three Hebrew men were hard pressed to violate God's command and bow down to an idol and worship it. They stood strong in their faith and were willing to die to obey God's word. Re-read and reflect on their responses to the king. What does it show you?

3. In Daniel 6, the Enemy goes after Daniel's prayer life. It would have been easy for Daniel to make excuses or adjustments or simply wait out the time. He does not. He understands the source of His strength is his time with God. Are you tenacious in protecting your prayer time?

4. In Daniel 10, we find principalities and powers of darkness ruling regions and opposing the work of God. Reflect on what the powers of darkness may be opposing in your life. Pray that God would bring breakthroughs in these areas.

Week 38

Reflection & Notes

Gratitude

Letters To God

My Letter:

His Reply:

Week 39

"But I am the Lord your God from the land of Egypt; you know no God but me, and besides me there is no savior." ~Hosea 13:4

READING PLAN

Day 1:	Hosea 1-4
Day 2:	Hosea 5-9
Day 3:	Hosea 10-14
Day 4:	Joel 1-3
Day 5:	Amos 1-5
Day 6:	Amos 6-9
Day 7:	Rest Day/Catch Up

Faith in Action

Ask someone in your life that you haven't always been patient with for forgiveness. You can try saying, "Please forgive me for not always being patient with you when I could have been."

Week 39   Date: _____

Journal Questions

1. The book of Hosea is a prophecy about the adultery of Israel. God likens our relationship with Him to a husband and wife. When Israel was walking out of line with God's ways, He told them they were in adultery. What picture does that give you for God's desire for us as His bride? How would you expect a faithful bride/wife to act, behave, think and treat you?

2. Are you acting like a faithful bride toward God? How can you improve in the ways that you show up in your relationship with God?

3. God is very patient with His people. He warns them numerous times and encourages them to come back to Him and His ways. He is a patient, loving Father. In what ways could you do a better job of being patient with the people in your life?

4. Are there times when God has given you a warning? Did you heed the warning? Why or why not? How can you improve in this area?

Week 39
Reflection & Notes

Gratitude

INSPIRATION

The Lord has healed me physically, spiritually, and emotionally many times, in many different ways.

I was a brand new Christian and had just been court-ordered to a Christian program. After being there for only a few days, we were playing volleyball at the church and I jumped up to hit the volleyball and heard a loud crack in my back. I fell to the ground in pain and I knew something had ruptured in my back.

At that time, I was on house arrest and was unable to go to the hospital without permission from my probation officer. It was a Saturday, so I was going to have to wait until Monday to get permission. That night I had a very hard time sleeping. It hurt to breathe, move, sit, and stand up. The next day at church, I told one of the ladies about it. She explained how she and two other ladies were going to pray a three-chord prayer over me for healing.

Honestly, I didn't really believe God would heal me because I was such a terrible person. The truth about grace, forgiveness and all that's available to us through salvation didn't really make sense to me yet.

The three ladies laid their hands on me. One of the ladies put her hand on the middle of my back where the pain was. As they began to pray, her hand started getting really hot. All of a sudden it was as if lightning shot from her hand through my back. I heard a bunch of cracking and popping and felt like there was fire in my back. When she was done, I was completely and totally healed! I was blown away. All I could say was, "Did you hear that? Oh my gosh, did you feel that your hand was on fire? My back was on fire!"

Those beautiful, mighty women smiled at me with a knowing smile and told me healing was part of my salvation. Jesus died so that I could be healed. His body was broken for me so that mine could be made whole. Since then, the Lord has healed me on many different occasions.

That day I discovered healing is real and healing is for now! Healing is for every born again believer, all daughters and sons of the living God. The Lord wants to heal us every single time we are in need. It is His will that we are healed. His Word says by His stripes we are healed. It does not say we were healed or we might be healed someday, but we are healed now! Psalm 103 says, "Jesus heals all of our sicknesses and diseases and He forgives all our iniquities. He makes us whole." Stand on His promises throughout the Word and see them manifest in your life. Step out in faith and be healed!

~Lynette Riganto

"Come, let us return to the Lord. He has torn us to pieces but he will heal us; he has injured us but he will bind up our wounds." ~Hosea 6:1

Week 40

"He has told you, O man, what is good; and what does the Lord require of you but to do justice, and to love kindness, and to walk humbly with your God?" ~*Micah 6:8*

READING PLAN

Day 1:	Obadiah 1
Day 2:	Jonah 1-4
Day 3:	Micah 1-4
Day 4:	Micah 5-7
Day 5:	Nahum 1-3
Day 6:	Habakkuk 1-3
Day 7:	Rest Day/Catch Up

Faith in Action

God created us to be a blessing. Find a way that you can be a blessing to someone this week.

Week 40 Date: _____

Journal Questions

1. Jonah tried to run away from what God was calling him to do. God made his path of travel difficult until Jonah repented and turned back to God and submitted to His will. Has there ever been a time in your life where you ran from what God was calling you to do? How did that turn out?

2. The prophets are the ones that heard from God often and would receive messages from Him to share. Sometimes, they wouldn't hear from Him for weeks, months, or years at a time. Have you experienced a time of "silence" from hearing God? How did you handle it?

3. When you feel as if you are not hearing from God, do you stop talking or asking Him things, or do you continue to press forward until you hear from Him?

4. Have there been times when you have given up hope in God answering you? Repent, ask Him to forgive you, and turn back to Him and His ways. He is a faithful friend.

Week 40
Reflection & Notes

Gratitude

Letters To God

My Letter:

His Reply:

Week 41

"The Lord your God is in your midst, a mighty one who will save; He will rejoice over you with gladness; He will quiet you by His love." ~Zephaniah 3:17

READING PLAN

Day 1:	Zephaniah 1-3
Day 2:	Haggai 1-2
Day 3:	Zechariah 1-5
Day 4:	Zechariah 6-10
Day 5:	Zechariah 11-14
Day 6:	Malachi 1-4
Day 7:	Rest Day/Catch Up

Faith in Action

Spend some time in prayer and walk through forgiving someone that has lied to you in the past that caused hurt, anger or bitterness. Forgive them, bless them, and release them. Do this just between you and God.

Week 41   Date: _____

Journal Questions

1. Look up the meaning of each of the prophet's names that we read this week and write them out below. For example, "Zechariah" means "God has remembered." There is meaning in the names of people that God uses.

2. How do you think these names correlate to what's written in the book of that prophet?

3. Malachi 3:6 tells us that God does not change. God is not like man that He should lie. He doesn't change. How does that make you feel? What confidence can you have in the One who will never change, or lie to you?

4. Chronologically, Malachi is the last book written before Jesus came, and then we were given the gospels. Could this book have significance in what's written? What is the message you've learned overall from what this prophet wrote?

Week 41
Reflection & Notes

Gratitude

Inspiration

On November 25th, 2021, my seventy-seven year old father was admitted to the hospital with covid pneumonia. He and my mother had both caught it and he went downhill very quickly. Five days later, he was intubated on a ventilator. On December 1st, the doctors told us he had one to seven days to live.

Family immediately flew in from all over. My husband watched the kids, and I spent my days at the hospital with my siblings.

A few days later, my 14 year old daughter, Jasna, asked me if she could come with me as I headed to my sister's house for the day. She was distraught and needed comfort. She had been with my parents when they got sick and was very close to them. I could tell she was shaken. I talked with her and prayed that the Holy Spirit would comfort her, give her peace, and let her know that He was with her.

A few minutes later, I received a text message that upset me so I decided to go home and rest. Jasna opted to stay at my sister's house, with everyone else.

Around 5pm, my siblings and Jasna were all praying together when suddenly, Jasna found herself in another room by herself. It was dark and there was a man standing in front of her. She didn't know who it was, but he spoke to her and said, "Everything is going to be okay."

She suddenly realized that it was Jesus in front of her! Just as suddenly, she was back in the room with everyone else. She began bawling and told them all what had happened.

A couple days later, we were told that my dad wouldn't make it more than a day. Days passed, and he was thankfully still alive.

December 26th, we got "the call" again to come and say goodbye. Ten of us went in and spent the day by his bedside praying. The doctor told us that he had irreparable brain damage, muscle wasting, and that his heart was starting to fail, and the compassionate thing to do would be to let him go.

My mom took several hours away to pray. She came back and decided to wait and see what happened.

The next day, a new doctor came in and examined my dad. He found nothing wrong with his heart!

My dad has since fully and completely recovered. He is able to take care of his own needs. He walks, talks, and has no sign of any brain damage! After 4 months in the hospital, he came home!

"See, I am YHWH, the Elohim of all flesh. Is there any matter too hard for Me?" Jeremiah 32:27

Not only did He heal my dad, but he comforted my daughter by showing up in-person to give her the message that everything would be okay. And He used this experience to strengthen our family in many ways.

~Rachel Pops

"And the angel said to those who were standing before him, 'Remove the filthy garments from him.' And to him he said, 'Behold, I have taken your iniquity away from you, and I will clothe you with pure vestments.'" ~Zechariah 3:4

Week 42

"Blessed are those who are persecuted for righteousness' sake, for theirs is the kingdom of heaven." ~*Matthew 5:10*

READING PLAN

Day 1:	Matthew 1-3
Day 2:	Matthew 4-7
Day 3:	Matthew 8-11
Day 4:	Matthew 12-15
Day 5:	Matthew 16-19
Day 6:	Matthew 20-22
Day 7:	Rest Day/Catch Up

Faith in Action

Add to the *Praise Report* in the back of this journal and give God some praise this week.

Week 42 Date: _____

Journal Questions

1. When Jesus was tried by the devil in the wilderness, He responded with scripture to any temptations thrown at Him. How can this be an example for us in our walk?

2. What's your first reaction when temptation or accusation comes your way? How can you start using scripture in your defense?

3. In Matthew 8, Jesus heals ten lepers and only one returns to Him to thank Him and give Him praise. That's just 10 percent! Are you quick to give God praise when He answers your prayers, or blesses you in some way? Do you lean toward the 10 percent camp of thanksgiving or the 90 percent that never returned with praise?

4. In Matthew 15:6-9, Jesus calls a group of Pharisees "hypocrites" and rebukes them for holding their man-made traditions over the Word of God. God sees our heart and knows our intentions. Are there any areas in your life where you appear one way but your heart is far from Him?

Week 42
Reflection & Notes

Gratitude

Letters To God

My Letter:

His Reply:

Week 43

"Watch and pray so that you will not fall into temptation. The spirit is willing, but the flesh is weak." ~*Mark 14:38*

READING PLAN

Day 1:	Matthew 23-25
Day 2:	Matthew 26-28
Day 3:	Mark 1-5
Day 4:	Mark 6-10
Day 5:	Mark 11-16
Day 6:	Luke 1-4
Day 7:	Rest Day/Catch Up

Faith in Action

Spend extra time in prayer this week. "Father, help me to see the areas I need to improve. Help my unbelief. Help me understand You and Your Word at a deeper level. Where am I falling short? Where do I need to increase my faith? You are good and worthy of all praise. Amen."

Week 43   Date: _____

Journal Questions

1. Jesus tells us to ask whatever we desire according to His will and to believe that we will receive it. What does it mean to pray "according to His will?"

2. Are you asking boldly for things in your prayers? In what ways could you improve this?

3. What comes out of our mouths is a reflection of our heart. Jesus rebuked the men for caring more about what they ate than how they spoke and acted (Mark 7:21-23). Are there any areas of the different defilements listed in these verses where you need improvement?

4. You are called to receive the reign of God as a little child. What does this mean? What does the faith of a child look like? In what ways could you walk with more child-like faith?

Week 43
Reflection & Notes

Gratitude

INSPIRATION

I have always been very active; enjoying running, roller skating, skiing, and weight lifting. I had just had my fifth child, a cute, cuddly little girl. I had four sons from my first marriage, so I was used to being a boys' mom. Having my first girl was so exciting. Right after Katie turned nine months, I began running again. Right around that same time, I started experiencing a horrible pain under my arm when she would nurse. I didn't think anything of it until the night after I ran my first mile, in almost a year. When I finished, I noticed I had this numbness in my side and around my stomach. The next morning, my left eye and the side of my mouth started twitching. Within a few days, the numbness had spread throughout my body.

Off to the clinic I went since I didn't have a doctor at the time. Thankfully, I was seen by an amazing female doctor. I told her my story and past history. She took my bloodwork. She called me in two days and said she got me an appointment with a Neurologist. At the time, that was a miracle. They were booked out and they just happened to have had a cancellation that Monday. At that appointment, he tested me and had me get an MRI the next day. He had me come in on Friday and told me that it was Multiple Sclerosis and I needed to get into the hospital immediately. As I was leaving to go home and pack, I had my friend take me to the store to buy a jogging suit, determined to not wear a hospital gown.

My hospital stay was like a party. I had so many friends and family come to visit, and so many flowers and phone calls. The down side was being hooked up to IVs for 10 days, 8 hours a day. I began to pray and declare, "Jesus is healing my body." Listening to the Bible on tape at night when I would go to sleep brought me peace and rest. His Word is the healing power of Jesus. Watching aerobics programs and sporting events was also a daily highlight. I felt God remind me of Proverbs 29:18, "Without a vision my people perish" and Proverbs 23:7, "As a man thinks in his heart so is he."

After I was released from the hospital, I went to a Naturopath and began a diet of very clean and healthy food. I realized the numbness was going away as I focused on the healing power of Jesus. He kept showing me how much He loved me. By that summer, I was water skiing again and in the winter I was skiing and back running and weightlifting. During this time, I was advised by my doctor to not have any more children as it could be hard on my body. God had other plans, and two years later, I had my sweet daughter, Angie. I worked out five days a week while pregnant with her, up until three days before she was born.

Twenty-two years later, I got a pinched nerve and went back to my original Neurologist. After some testing, he said, "If you came to me and said you had MS, I would not believe you even though I am the doctor who diagnosed you. You have no signs of it at all." Praise God for His healing power!

~Maureen Brundage

Week 44

"Strive to enter through the narrow door. For many, I tell you, will seek to enter and will not be able." ~Luke 13:24

READING PLAN

Day 1:	Luke 5-7
Day 2:	Luke 8-11
Day 3:	Luke 12-14
Day 4:	Luke 15-18
Day 5:	Luke 19-21
Day 6:	Luke 22-24
Day 7:	Rest Day/Catch Up

Faith in Action

Jesus commands His followers to be quick to forgive and to forgive "seventy times seven." What unforgiveness are you storing up in your heart against someone? Do you need to call them, text them or write them a letter releasing them from the bitterness you have against them? Or maybe just pray and forgive them. Unforgiveness keeps you trapped and a "prisoner." It's time to forgive.

Week 44   Date: _____

Journal Questions

1. Jesus asked his followers to leave everything and follow Him. What do you think He meant by that? What might it mean for you to "leave everything" and follow Him?

2. Is there something you need to "leave" to follow Him? What is He asking you to surrender and leave behind?

3. When we put our belief and trust in the Son, our sin is forgiven. Are there places you need to forgive others with the same compassion that God has shown to you?

4. In Luke 12:22, Jesus said to His disciples, "Do not worry about your life." When we worry, we are not walking in faith. What worries do you have that you are ready to surrender to God so you can live in more faith?

Week 44
Reflection & Notes

Gratitude

Letters To God

My Letter:

His Reply:

Week 45

"But the hour is coming, and is now here, when the true worshipers will worship the Father in spirit and truth, for the Father is seeking such people to worship Him." ~John 4:23

READING PLAN

Day 1: John 1-4
Day 2: John 5-8
Day 3: John 9-11
Day 4: John 12-15
Day 5: John 16-18
Day 6: John 19-21
Day 7: Rest Day/Catch Up

Faith in Action

Help someone in need. Pray for a stranger that God lays on your heart.

Week 45   Date: _____

Journal Questions

1. John 3:14 mentions the serpent in the wilderness that Moses held up. How were the people in the wilderness healed? How does that relate to what John is saying about Jesus in this scripture?

2. John 12:23 says, "They loved the praise of men more than the praise of God." Are you guilty of this? Do you fall into the trap of worrying more about what man believes, and praises you for, than God? What shift will you make to improve this?

3. How can you stay in the "True Vine?" Reread what it says in John 15 and journal about it.

4. John talks about how men loved darkness more than the light because their deeds were evil. What does "darkness" represent? Is there any "darkness" in your life that you are harboring that God wants you to release?

Week 45

Reflection & Notes

Gratitude

INSPIRATION

I was raised Jewish. In the 1990's, I moved from New York City to Hawaii for graduate school. While there, I learned about the Jewish Messiah, Jesus, and how He fulfilled all of the prophecies I learned about while growing up. I was so excited to share my faith with others and started to do so when a Japanese friend of mine invited me to meet at the local hospital to pray for the sick. I had never done this before.

We walked down the halls praying and we felt God lead us to a room with a sick father. He was hooked up to machines and was unconscious. His two daughters and wife were in the room crying. We circled his bed, held hands, and began to pray. As we were praying, I heard the still small voice of God prompt me to prophesy the man would be healed in three days. I told one daughter and she became angry. She said, "My father is about to die. How can you say such a thing?" The other daughter said she believed, and prayed with us for this to happen.

The next day, we returned and witnessed a miracle. He was able to move his shoulder and other parts of his body. The daughters and mother got on their knees and prayed fervently. Shortly after, they purchased Bibles. The following day I came in to pray for him again, and his eyes were open. He was still hooked up to a heart machine and kept trying to get the tubes out of his throat. The doctor said, "This is a miracle. He should not be alive. He had a ten percent chance of living." I told the doctor I am not surprised because I prayed to Jesus and He answered the prayer.

The third day, I did not return, but I received a phone call from my friend who said he had been moved to a different floor and was no longer in the ICU. I came back on the fourth day and met many more of his family members. They were all smiling from ear to ear, glowing. They all purchased Bibles. Their father reached out to take my hand. He was healed! We continued to go to the prayer chapel to pray with family members. We saw many more miracles.

Another miracle that really stuck out to me happened when we decided to walk down the hall and ask God where He wanted to take us. We felt led to enter a room. To my surprise, one of my clients, who I had been praying for, was in this room. His grandmother was dying. She was Japanese and a Buddhist. My friend, who was with me, had converted from Buddhism to Christianity and was able to explain to her the good news that Jesus takes away sins in Japanese. The next time I saw him he had told all my coworkers the testimony of his grandmother's salvation and healing.

God's miracles may be waiting on our "yes!"

~Rhonda Gordon

"Now Jesus did many other signs in the presence of the disciples, which are not written in this book; 31 but these are written so that you may believe that Jesus is the Christ, the Son of God, and that by believing you may have life in his name." ~John 20:30-31

Week 46

"Repent and be baptized every one of you in the name of Jesus Christ for the forgiveness of your sins, and you will receive the gift of the Holy Spirit." ~Acts 2:38

READING PLAN

Day 1:	Acts 1-3
Day 2:	Acts 4-7
Day 3:	Acts 8-10
Day 4:	Acts 11-14
Day 5:	Acts 15-17
Day 6:	Acts 18-21
Day 7:	Rest Day/Catch Up

Faith in Action

Do something bold to share the love of Jesus with others this week.

Week 46 Date: _____

Journal Questions

1. When the apostles received the promise of the Holy Spirit on Shavuot (pentecost), how many were saved that day? (Acts 2:41) Go back and read the account in Exodus 32:8 about the golden calf incident. How many died that day? Do you see any similarities?

2. Stephen was a bold apostle for Christ. Read his account of Jesus in Acts 7. Why was he killed? Did his death shock you?

3. What are some things you notice about the body of believers in Acts? What do you see that we could improve upon today as the body of Christ?

4. What are two ways you were challenged in the readings this week? Is there an area you can improve in your walk of faith as modeled by the apostles? What actions will you take?

Week 46
Reflection & Notes

Gratitude

Letters To God

My Letter:

His Reply:

Week 47

"Do not be conformed to this world, but be transformed by the renewal of your mind, that by testing you may discern what is the will of God, what is good and acceptable and perfect." ~Romans 2:12

READING PLAN

Day 1:	Acts 22-25
Day 2:	Acts 26-28
Day 3:	Romans 1-4
Day 4:	Romans 5-8
Day 5:	Romans 9-12
Day 6:	Romans 13-16
Day 7:	Rest Day/Catch Up

Faith in Action

Pray and ask God to reveal to you in what ways you are still walking in the flesh. Repent and turn back to His ways. Give Him praise for the ways in which He has helped you to walk according to His Spirit!

Week 47 Date: _____

Journal Questions

1. Paul talks about the constant battle of walking in the flesh versus the Spirit. What does it look like to walk in the flesh? What does it look like to walk in the Spirit?

2. Romans 11 talks about how the gentile nations were grafted into the olive tree. It's a powerful imagery given to us to show how God took us into His root and allowed us to be grafted in as if we were naturally born into the root. What does this "grafting in" look like? What does it mean for those "grafted in?"

3. Romans 12:12 says, "Do not conform to this world but be transformed by the renewing of your mind." How can you apply this to your life? Why is it important in your walk with God?

4. Paul defines the law as good and necessary. Without it (the law or Torah), we wouldn't know where we need to improve and that we are in desperate need of a Savior. Where did you "come from" that you needed Jesus as your Savior? How did you know you needed Him? What did He save you from?

Week 47

Reflection & Notes

Gratitude

Inspiration

For 16 years, I reacted to eating gluten. In third grade, I went to the nurses office with a headache almost everyday. My mother picked me up from school early for weeks before we finally figured out that the culprit was gluten. We immediately cut it out of my diet almost completely. This was just the beginning of gluten taking things from me.

As I got older, the symptoms steadily grew worse. What began as a simple headache and an inability to sit through math class, turned into migraines that forced me to go home and lay in bed in a dark room. I threw up at a friend's birthday dinner because the restaurant cross-contaminated my meal and I didn't realize I had eaten gluten. My symptoms eventually evolved into flu-like body aches that lasted an entire week after I'd been "glutened."

Eventually, I went completely gluten free, but that still didn't solve my health problems and it caused me to miss out on so many experiences. I felt guilt and shame every time I went over to friends' houses and carefully investigated every meal or snack they made for me, in order to make sure I wouldn't get sick. Although I had a lot of options for gluten free meals, a strict gluten-free lifestyle took the joy and excitement away from meeting up with friends, attending birthday parties, and traveling. I lived with fear in the back of my mind that something I ate would put me in physical pain and cause me to miss out on all the fun. I don't believe we were created to only enjoy life halfway.

A year ago, a friend shared on Instagram that she was miraculously healed of Celiac Disease and Hashimoto's. As I read her post, I thought, "God, why is that possible for her and not for me?" He responded with an answer I didn't expect. "Why is it not possible for you?" I was not ready to go there, but every couple of months I thought about her story. If she could be healed then maybe it was possible for me. I don't remember what exactly changed for me, but in November I decided that I was tired of being gluten-free. I saw some of my friends eating a cinnamon roll, my favorite Saturday morning breakfast as a child, and got frustrated with the fact that I couldn't eat them. I wanted my own healing.

In December, I attended a conference at my church and I knew that healing was for me and it was happening that day. During prayer time, I ran up to a lady and asked her, "Will you pray with me that my celiac is gone and the fear doesn't hold me back any longer?" We prayed and I got exactly what I asked. I was able to take communion with the rest of the church for the first time in seven years. Since then, I can eat as much gluten as I want. I wasn't able to eat bread for most of my life. Now, I have so much joy, excitement, and gratitude. I no longer feel stress or fear when I travel. I get to celebrate birthdays without adjusting what I eat. I had read about all the miraculous stories of healings throughout the Bible, but for some reason I had forgotten that He is still doing healing miracles today!

~Mary DeAcetis

"As it is written, 'I have made you the father of many nations'—in the presence of the God in whom he believed, who gives life to the dead and calls into existence the things that do not exist." ~Romans 4:17

Week 48

"Love is patient and kind; love does not envy or boast; it is not arrogant." ~1 Corinthians 13:4

READING PLAN

Day 1:	1 Corinthians 1-4
Day 2:	1 Corinthians 5-8
Day 3:	1 Corinthians 9-12
Day 4:	1 Corinthians 13-16
Day 5:	2 Corinthians 1-6
Day 6:	2 Corinthians 7-13
Day 7:	Rest Day/Catch Up

Faith in Action

We live in a broken and fallen world and small acts of kindness can mean so much to others. Ask God how you can step up and show kindness to a stranger this week. Perhaps something as simple as buying the coffee of the person in line behind you at Starbucks and saying, "God bless you!"

Week 48 Date: _____

Journal Questions

1. The Apostle Paul, brings a lot of correction and clarification about what it means to be a member of the Body of Messiah. There are many roles for many members. We get to embrace our individual role and gifts. What is your role in the body? What gifts do you bring?

2. 2 Corinthians 5:18 talks to us about the "new man." We become a new creation when we are in our Savior, Jesus. What is the "new man" and what does that represent in Jesus? What is the "old man" and what does that represent?

3. Paul had a "thorn in his side." (2 Corinthians 12) We are not told what the "thorn" is, but rather that it was some sort of hardship or pain, either physical or spiritual. Perhaps we are not told so that we are able to bring whatever hardship we are suffering in the place of this story. What hardship or struggles has God walked you through?

4. His grace is sufficient for you. His power is made perfect in your weakness. How can you find comfort in God's grace alone?

Week 48
Reflection & Notes

Gratitude

Letters To God

My Letter:

His Reply:

Week 49

"I can do all things through Him who strengthens me."
~Philippians 4:13

READING PLAN

Day 1:	Galatians 1-6
Day 2:	Ephesians 1-6
Day 3:	Philippians 1-4
Day 4:	Colossians 1-4
Day 5:	1 Thessalonians 1-5
Day 6:	2 Thessalonians 1-3
Day 7:	Rest Day/Catch Up

Faith in Action

Put on the full Armor of God. Read Ephesians 6:11-18 out loud every day this week.

Week 49   Date: _____

Journal Questions

1. As believers, we are challenged to die to our flesh daily. Our flesh brings corruption, old patterns, and sin. What are the workings of the flesh mentioned in Galatians? What are the workings of the Spirit? What "flesh" do you still need to put to death? What workings of the Spirit can you pray for?

2. Compare the Armor of God (Ephesians 6: 11-18) to the Levitical priesthood garments (Exodus 28: 2-42). Some people think there is a correlation. What do you think?

3. What is something you had to let go of from your past to help you move forward as a believer and deepen your relationship with God?

4. Read and meditate on Ephesians 2. It is your adoption story. You are adopted into the citizenship of spiritual Israel. What does that mean to you?

Week 49
Reflection & Notes

Gratitude

Inspiration

I was a homeschool mom of nine children, pregnant with the tenth. There was a lot going on in my life, and one very difficult situation really consumed me. The storms raging around me started to impact me internally, creating a storm within. Nine babies in eighteen years and lots of sleepless nights had taken a toll on my mind and body.

When I was thinking hard about something, trying to figure it out on my own, I would start to feel like I was spinning and my eyes would roll back. I went to see a naturopathic doctor. She checked my pulse and immediately applied acupuncture. When she came back to the room after about twenty minutes, she said, "When you came in, you were on the verge of a Grand Mal Seizure." That seemed to explain why I wasn't feeling well.

I left the office that day trusting God with my next steps concerning the news I had received. This doctor closed her office shortly after that visit. It wasn't even an option to see her again and I did not plan to see another doctor about this illness. I felt led to work through this problem another way. As a daughter of God, I wanted to trust in the Spirit's leading and not lean of my own understanding this time. I brought the diagnosis to God and asked Him what He wanted to do about it.

When I would feel overwhelmed, the spinning would come on. My two older daughters would help with the other children so I could be alone in my room. Then I would lay down on my bed, where it was dark and quiet, and pray in the Spirit, in tongues to be specific. At that point in my life I didn't have the mind to come up with my own words to form a prayer, so praying in tongues was such a gift. This allowed me to pray with my prayer language from my spirit. God would strengthen me from that place. Totally relaxing my mind and casting all my cares on Him was crucial. I needed to roll all the anxieties and fears on Him so I could get well. I purposefully cleared my mind and allowed only the word of God to flow through my thoughts. I would declare, "No weapon formed against me shall prosper. By Your stripes I am healed." while laying in bed. By faith, I believed His words would come to pass.

My prayer time would take about a half an hour. Then I would get up and continue my normal routine with the family. This routine continued for about two weeks. By the end of the two weeks, the spinning had subsided enough so I didn't need to lay down anymore. Light spinning continued occasionally for another year or so. It was so minimal that it didn't interrupt my daily life at all. I just kept believing "I am healed, and this can't stay."

Finally, all spinning subsided, and I was completely healed! I praise God for His healing hand in my life. Hebrews 4:12 says, "The Word of God is alive and active, and sharper than a double-edged sword." Stand on His Word and apply it to your life. When you do, expect miracles!

~Jackie Dighans

Week 50

"But we do not belong to those who shrink back and are destroyed, but to those who have faith and are saved." ~*Hebrews 10:39*

READING PLAN

Day 1:	1 Timothy 1-6
Day 2:	2 Timothy 1-4
Day 3:	Titus 1-3
Day 4:	Philemon 1-Hebrews 4
Day 5:	Hebrews 5-9
Day 6:	Hebrews 10-13
Day 7:	Rest Day/Catch Up

Faith in Action

Pray and ask God to help your unbelief and show you blind spots in your faith so that you can be strengthened in your walk with Him.

Week 50 Date: _____

Journal Questions

1. 1 Timothy 4:10 tells us to "fix our hope on the living God, who is the Savior of all the people, especially those who believe." How can you fix your hope in Him in this season of your life?

2. What does it look like to walk in a spirit of "power, love and self control?" (2 Timothy 1:7)

3. What can be some of the goals you can have for yourself based on what is referenced in Titus 2?

4. In Hebrews 11 we are given examples of stories of great faith. What stands out to you about the faith of these people? How is your faith today? In what ways have your hardships or trials in life grown your faith?

Week 50
Reflection & Notes

Gratitude

Letters To God

My Letter:

His Reply:

Week 51

"But in your hearts honor Christ the Lord as holy, always being prepared to make a defense to anyone who asks you for a reason for the hope that is in you; yet do it with gentleness and respect."
~1 Peter 3:15

READING PLAN

Day 1:	James 1-5
Day 2:	1 Peter 1-5
Day 3:	2 Peter 1-3
Day 4:	1 John 1-5
Day 5:	2 John 1, 3 John 1
Day 6:	Jude 1
Day 7:	Rest Day/Catch Up

Faith in Action

Take some time to self-reflect through the readings this week. Pray and seek God in areas you need to let go, things that need to not be a part of your walk, and things to add to your walk with Him.

Week 51   Date: _____

Journal Questions

1. James talks about how our belief in Jesus leads us into good works. What are "good works" as defined in scripture?

2. How can you apply those "good works" in your everyday life?

3. What is "sin" as it is defined in scripture? (1 John 3) With that definition, how should we recognize "sin" in ourselves and repent? Read it in multiple translations to study it more in depth.

4. The scriptures we read this week all seem to talk about the potential of "falling away." It's mentioned often, which makes it seem like a warning of relevance. According to this week's reading, what does "falling away" from faith or God look like? What can you do to keep that from happening to you?

Week 51
Reflection & Notes

Gratitude

Inspiration

I was raised in a Catholic Church, where I was baptized, had my communion, and my confirmation. After my parents' divorce, my family stepped away from the church. I went off to college and found an easy money job in a gentlemen's club, where I sold my soul for eleven years. In order to do what I did, I numbed myself with alcohol and a variety of drugs. I had my first son at twenty-eight and was clean the entire pregnancy.

I thought I was done, but eventually slipped back to filling the empty hole in my soul with all the wrong things. In 2017, when my son was four, I was arrested for possession. This was the best thing that could ever happen to me and I mean it! I got a scholarship into a treatment program where I stayed for 93 days. At that treatment program I found God, the right people, discovered meditation and tools to stop my cravings. God filled the hole in my soul!

I began a new relationship after leaving treatment with a man I thought was my soulmate. We had a son together in 2020, who we named Tommy. Unbeknownst to me, my son's father was a narcissist and showed me exactly what I wanted to see. Four months later, he was in jail. He came back when Tommy was 10-months-old. I hoped he'd be different, but on Valentine's morning 2022, I realized he wasn't.

I had taken my older son to school and left him home with the baby while I went to work. At 10:24am I had this gut feeling that something was not right. I called and texted for an hour with no answer, so I told my boss I needed to run home. I know now this was the Holy Spirit prompting me to go home right away. I found my now ex-fiancé passed out, laying on top of our 18-month-old son. There was drug paraphernalia on the floor. The baby was purple and not breathing. The ambulance took him away, lifeless. I wasn't sure if he ingested any drugs, but there was because there was white foam around his mouth and when we gave him CPR he threw up. He was flown to a Children's hospital and placed on a ventilator for five days.

For those five days I prayed hard. A wise woman in Bible study told me, "Prayer activates the armor of God." So, I called close friends and family and many prayer chains were formed. A local friend organized a prayer service at a church where I cried my eyes out watching from the hospital on FB live. Tommy had an army praying for him. His MRI showed scattered brain damage to his cerebellum. Once he began to awaken from all the meds, the fear struck. Would he crawl, walk, chew, or speak again? Would he have cerebral palsy? These were the possibilities the doctors mentioned due to the oxygen deprivation in the area of his brain that was damaged. I stayed by Tommy's side, holding his hand and praying.

Miraculously, by God's grace and through faith, my baby was restored! Tommy left the hospital after ten days. He is walking and eating on his own, and speaking the way he was before the incident. I've been taking the boys to church. I want to reaffirm our faith in Christ and have us all baptized. We are forever grateful and give praise to the Lord for His unfailing love & faithfulness. We believe He has great plans in store for our future.

~Nicole Campanelli

Week 52

"And they overcame him by the blood of the Lamb, and by the word of their testimony; and they loved not their lives unto death."
~*Revelation 12:11*

READING PLAN

Day 1:	Revelation 1-3
Day 2:	Revelation 4-7
Day 3:	Revelation 8-11
Day 4:	Revelation 12-15
Day 5:	Revelation 16-19
Day 6:	Revelation 20-22
Day 7:	Rest Day/Catch Up

Faith in Action

Pray this prayer: "Father, thank you for Your set apart Word that has filled me up and is alive and active. You are the Creator of all things and I thank you today for the ability that I have to sit and read Your Word every day. Thank you for giving me the strength and endurance to read Your entire Word. Praise You! All glory and esteem is Yours forever and ever. Amen!"

Week 52 Date: _____

Journal Questions

1. Our testimony holds power. How do you define "testimony?" What is your testimony?

2. In Revelation 2-3, we find Jesus in the midst of the local church. The churches had their issues, but Jesus was still there. How are you doing in being a part of and serving in a local church family, or in your community?

3. Revelation is a book to help our hearts and minds prepare for the return of our Messiah. Are you prepared? How can you be more prepared and joyfully anticipating His return?

4. YOU DID IT! Now that you have finished, write out how you are feeling about accomplishing this goal of reading the Bible cover to cover!

Week 52
Reflection & Notes

Gratitude

Letters To God

My Letter:

His Reply:

Walk In His Ways

Are you going to experience heaven for eternity with our Savior? If your answer is "yes," praise God!

If you're not sure, you *can* be sure. First - repent. You've now read His whole Word and you have a much better understanding of what He seeks in His children. You have fallen short. We all have. Repent of your sin. To repent means to turn away from sin and to turn to God. So turn today.

Repenting looks like: Asking for forgiveness. He's willing and ready to forgive you today. Just ask Him! "Father forgive me for…"

Now choose to walk in His ways, everyday. Ask Him to be Lord of your life and King in your heart. His answer will be "Yes!" Will you mess up again? Yep! Just repent, friend. Every time. Repent, and turn back.

There will be a time for every knee to know Him and bow. Choose Him. He's worthy. He's worth it.

Celebrate! You Did It!

You completed reading the entire Bible cover to cover!

Take a picture with your Bible and give Him all the praise for this accomplishment.

Invite others to join you and start again. Everyday we get to choose Him and His Word.

Now that you have finished, we'd love to read what this journal and study has done for you! Email us at: *stories@StudyHisWord.com*.

Prayer Log

Date	Name	Prayer Request

Copyright © 2022 Fear Into Faith Incorporated

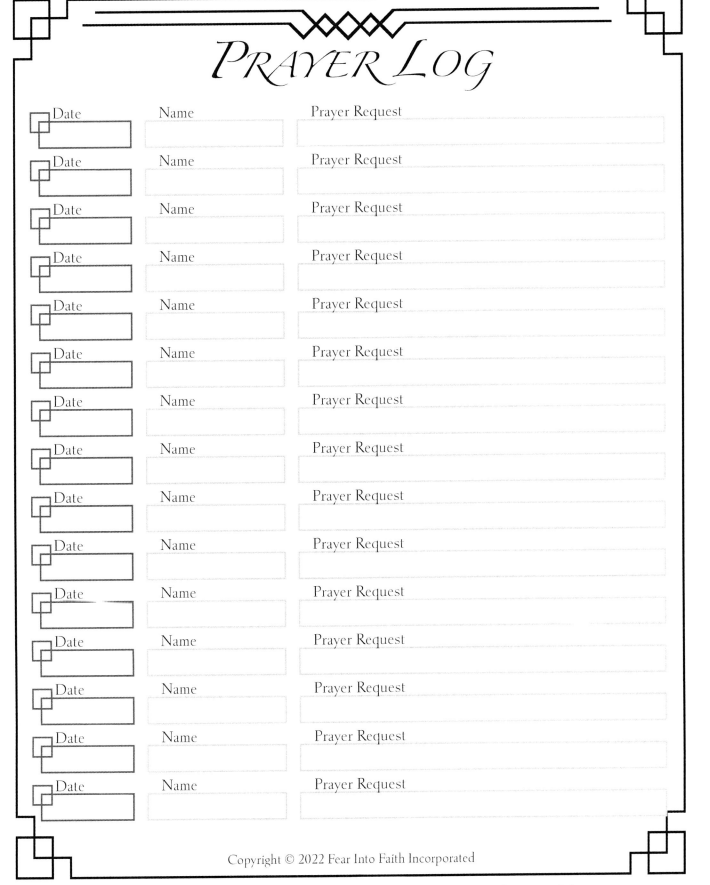

Praise Report

Date	Praise Report

Copyright © 2022 Fear Into Faith Incorporated

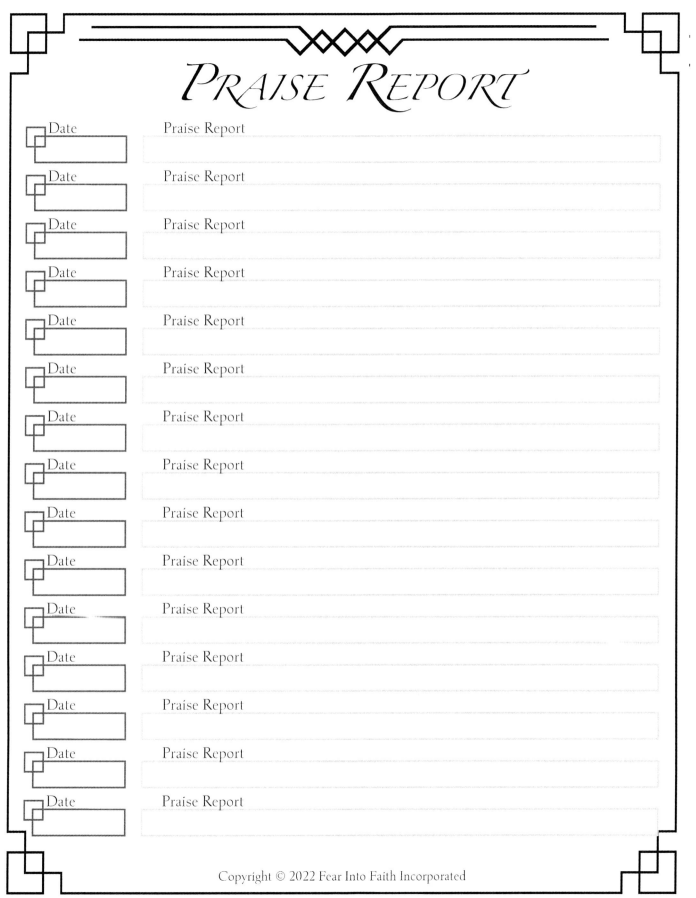

NOTES

Save the Date!

September 16-17, 2023

End of the Year Celebration

We want to celebrate with you when you finish reading the Bible cover to cover. In 2023, we will celebrate with men and women on September 16-17th. (Location to be determined.) At this event, we will get the opportunity to finish reading the last part of the book of Revelation together, which will be a POWERFUL moment you won't want to miss! We would love to have you there.

Visit **www.StudyHisWord.com** for more info.

Would you like to receive future books from Kingdom Mindset Publishing absolutely free?

We like to give away free copies of our books each month!

We could use your help.

God is calling us to create more Bible study guides in the near future. We would appreciate hearing your thoughts on this 52-Week Bible Study Guide. Your feedback will assist us in improving the next round of books with sections, guides, and resources you would like to see. We have put together a brief 2-minute survey.

To be entered into our monthly drawing, simply fill out the survey at:
www.StudyHisWord.com/survey

More From Kingdom Mindset Publishing

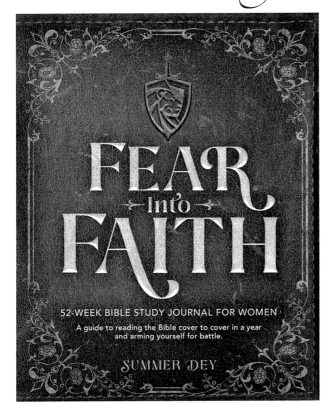
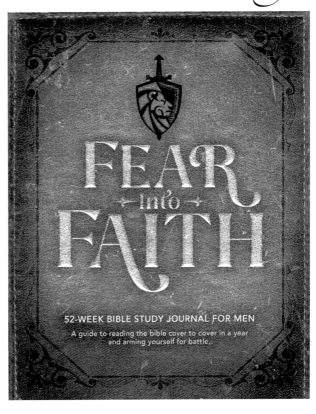

"Finally, be strong in the Lord and in the strength of His might. Put on the whole armor of God, that you may be able to stand against the schemes of the devil." ~Ephesians 6:10-11

There is no greater tool to arm God's people against the schemes of the Enemy than for them to be in the Word of God each and every day. We are excited to offer you the **Fear Into Faith: 52-Week Bible Study Journal for Women** and **Fear Into Faith: 52-Week Bible Study Journal for Men**, for those who want more tools to study His Word. It is time for us to be in His Word, to put on the armor of God each and every day, and to lead our families as God has called us to.

www.StudyHisWord.com

Inspirational Stories

- ~Maya Baker 20
- ~Nikki Cruise 28
- ~Jamie Gatchell 36
- ~Stacy McLain 44
- ~Jayme Berube 52
- ~Dr. Richard Yarbrough 60
- ~Summer Dey 68
- ~Todd Jones 76
- ~Marilyn Sadlier 84
- ~Nancy Ann Johnson 92
- ~Paul Nandico 100
- ~Ben Miller 108
- ~Michelle Rene' Hammer 116
- ~Apostle Jessica Z. Maldonado 124
- ~Dafne Wiswell 132
- ~Jennifer Loza 140
- ~Brit Coppa 148
- ~Caroline Duocher 156
- ~Terri Adwell 164
- ~Lynette Riganto 172
- ~Rachel Pops 180
- ~Maureen Brundage 188
- ~Rhonda Gordon 196
- ~Mary DeAcetis 204
- ~Jackie Dighans 212
- ~Nicole Campanelli 220

Before You Go!

We have a gift we would like to give to you!

We hope you have enjoyed your journey through the Bible cover to cover. We know the importance of not only studying His Word, but also the importance of memorizing scripture verses and having them in places where you will see them often.

We have created special Bible verse cards with the 52 verses found in each week of this journal. We would like to bless you with them.

"Who performs wonders that cannot be fathomed, miracles that cannot be counted."
~ Job 5:9

Go to <u>www.StudyHisWord.com/gift</u> to print off your free Bible verse cards.

You can put them up around your home, carry them in your wallet, give them as gifts, etc. We pray they will be a powerful reminder of the time you have spent in His Word and what His promises are to you.

"Let the word of Christ dwell in you richly, teaching and admonishing one another in all wisdom, singing psalms and hymns and spiritual songs, with thankfulness in your hearts to God." ~Colossians 3:16

About the Journal Creator

SUMMER DEY is an International Speaker and Success Coach who helps people from around the globe shift FEAR into FAITH. She has spoken to, and motivated, thousands on platforms all over the world. She uses her voice and her influence to "set captives free" and to take back territories for the Kingdom.

She is the proud Proverbs 31 wife of Marcelo and a homeschooling mother of three beautiful warriors. In 2020, they sold all of their belongings to "pick up their mat and walk," and moved into an RV to travel around the country and serve wherever God calls them.

www.SummerDey.com

Pastoral & Biblical Advisor

JEREMY ANTHONY is a charismatic, compassionate pastor with a desire to see people discover their destiny in Christ through teaching, discipleship, and the practical application of God's Word. Born in Minnesota, but raised in New Zealand, he has completed multiple degrees in computer science, Bible and missions. He has served as a youth pastor, church planter, lead pastor, and executive pastor. His passion for God's word comes from his father who was a pastor, missionary and bible school teacher. He and his incredible wife, Kariann, have three wonderful kids, all of whom are his priority and joy.